SUSTAINABILITY AND POVERTY OUTREACH IN MICROFINANCE: THE SRI LANKAN EXPERIENCE

SUSTAINABILITY AND POVERTY OUTREACH IN MICROFINANCE: THE SRI LANKAN EXPERIENCE

TO RESOLVE DILEMMAS OF MICROFINANCE PRACTITIONERS AND POLICY MAKERS

H AMARATHUNGA

SUSTAINABILITY AND POVERTY OUTREACH IN MICROFINANCE: THE SRI LANKAN EXPERIENCE

TO RESOLVE DILEMMAS OF MICROFINANCE PRACTITIONERS AND POLICY MAKERS

iUniverse books may be ordered through booksellers or by contacting:

iUniverse
1663 Liberty Drive
Bloomington, IN 47403
www.iuniverse.com
1-800-Authors (1-800-288-4677)

Because of the dynamic nature of the Internet, any web addresses or links contained in this book may have changed since publication and may no longer be valid. The views expressed in this work are solely those of the author and do not necessarily reflect the views of the publisher, and the publisher hereby disclaims any responsibility for them.

Any people depicted in stock imagery provided by Getty Images are models, and such images are being used for illustrative purposes only. Certain stock imagery © Getty Images.

ISBN: 978-1-5320-7931-3 (sc)
ISBN: 978-1-5320-7930-6 (e)

Library of Congress Control Number: 2019911180

Print information available on the last page.

iUniverse rev. date: 08/16/2019

"The best way to find yourself is to lose yourself in the service of others."

—Gandhi

CONTENTS

LIST OF TABLES

LIST OF FIGURES

FOREWORD

This book titled Sustainability and Poverty Outreach in Microfinance: The Sri Lankan Experience is a result of research carried out by the author, Dr. Hituhamulage Amarathunga, for his doctoral thesis at the Faculty of Graduate Studies, University of Colombo, Sri Lanka. The study mainly focuses on the financial sustainability of the micro finance institutions (MFIs) as a strategy for poverty reduction in Sri Lanka. The scope of the study has been expanded to analyze the impact of financial and non-financial variables, including the group-based lending in comparison with individual-based lending, on the financial performance of MFIs.

Empirical evidence shows that the services provided by the MFIs to the poor are allied with significant challenges, which are not common to many other formal financial institutions. Small-sized loans granted by MFIs carry a large proportion of processing cost while the lack of creditworthiness of the clients, resulting mainly from the absence of collateral, managerial and entrepreneurial capacity is common. Therefore, the default risk of such loans is naturally high, and the sustainability of MFIs is low. In this backdrop, the expected contribution of MFIs to serve the poor without a strong financial foundation is a matter for concern.

In the above context, analytical presentation of the book ushers the reader through the current debate on sustainability versus poverty outreach of MFIs in Sri Lanka. Having collected data and information relevant to 50 MFIs in Sri Lanka for a six-year time span, the study delved into question the extent to which these MFIs have succeeded in maintaining financial sustainability in relation to depth of poverty outreach. Further, the research has focused on the question as to how lending methods adopted by MFIs in Sri Lanka affect their own sustainability and/or depth of poverty outreach. Answers to this question can be viewed in the context of identifying the influence that different types of lending methods adopted by the MFIs can have on the cost and efficiency of their operations. The study also emphasizes the relationship of poverty outreach with such variables as operational self-sufficiency (OSS), employment of female loan officers, number of branches and volume of assets/loans of MFIs.

The main objective of the research focuses on the possible trade-off (or compatibility) between sustainability and poverty outreach of MFIs in Sri Lanka. The specific objectives include the understanding of key operational variables that can make significant impact on outreach efforts of MFIs to serve disadvantaged and vulnerable groups in the society. Further, the investigation and analysis of the lending methods adopted by MFIs is carried out to provide insights into the formulation of lending operations best suited to achieve improved financial status for the MFIs operating in Sri Lanka.

There is a positive relationship between the operational self-sufficiency of MFIs and the depth of poverty outreach according to the main findings of the study. Moreover, these results indicate that servicing to the poor by MFIs has not caused any adverse impact on MFIs' financial performance. The implementation of group lending schemes has helped the MFIs to build up a long-term and strong relationships with clients.

The findings further suggest that the size of the asset portfolio of an MFI affects poverty outreach positively reflecting the fact that MFIs have made use of their assets/funds productively. The female loan officers are more efficient in maintaining close interact with clients rather than their male counterparts according to the findings. This strategy is useful to maintain high recovery rates of MFIs loans. MFIs can reach to the poor clients efficiently with the expansion of their branch networks and the augmenting of their equity funds.

Many MFIs in Sri Lanka are operating with low capital base now, so that these institutions are facing financial challenges in service coverage and diversification of their products. The promoting of group lending practice are useful in this endeavor as it reduces average lending/ borrowing cost, enhances financial sustainability, and promotes formal lending/borrowing culture among poor communities. This would also be useful to reduce rural indebtedness and related poverty issues in the country.

The study findings emphasize the necessity to adopt a conducive policy framework to empower the MFIs to achieve sustainable and inclusive financial culture in the country. Under performing MFIs are not able to serve the people to reduce poverty effectively. Among others, such policy issues as proper targeting of poverty groups, expansion of joint liability schemes for collateral free lending, increase of assets, broad based equity capital, high percentage of female loan officers and the expansion of branch network would produce the desired results.

The research suggests that the compilation of data about the operations of MFIs in the country is a difficult exercise, mainly due to many MFIs do not keep records properly as there is no mandatory requirement to do so according to the regulatory mechanism. On the other hand, MFIs which come under some form of government involvement have ignored in pursuing of administrative and financial regulations. Such issues seem to have restricted the sample to 50 MFIs of this study. Similarly, the information on such MFIs were collected from multiple sources complicating the issues further. However, such limitations have not affected the overall quality of the study and its conclusion.

In the past, the global poverty level has declined to a greater extent, although there are still around eight hundred million people might be living under poverty. They need the financial support to come out of the poverty and MFIs are instrumental in this endeavor. However, MFIs will not function efficiently unless there is an appropriate link between the financial sustainability and poverty outreach. In the light of capacity possessed by MFIs, this study provides new insights in addressing global poverty through microfinance facilities.

The researcher has done an outstanding job under a number of constraints and his findings are useful in formulating microfinance policies not only in Sri Lanka but also in many other developing countries. This research will also open the flood gates for further research in microfinance in Sri Lanka and elsewhere.

Rev. Prof. Wijitapure Wimalaratana,
Department of Economics, University of Colombo
Sri Lanka

PREFACE

It is widely believed that the main objective of microfinance institutions (MFIs) is to provide financial services to the poor to bring about a favorable impact on their income and poverty levels. MFIs accordingly adopt different approaches to reach the poor, resulting in different levels of success in terms of achieving depth of poverty outreach and their own sustainability. In this context, this book mainly evaluates the extent to which MFIs in Sri Lanka have been successful in maintaining financial sustainability versus reaching the poor. Besides, the book also investigates the effectiveness of certain lending methods adopted by MFIs on their financial success.

It is observed through the data analysis that sustainability of MFIs has a positive relationship with poverty outreach and there is no evidence that MFIs pursue financial goals at the expense of social performance. Our analyses further show, inter alia, that expansion of branch network, employment of female loan officers and increase of asset/loan portfolio by MFIs result in a favorable impact on reaching the poor. According to the study, MFIs which adopt group-based lending extensively, make headway over individual-based lending in achieving operational self-sufficiency. In this context, it can be concluded that sustainability of the MFIs also differs according to the lending methods adopted by them.

Experience of MFIs in Sri Lanka suggest that pursuit of sustainability disregarding poverty outreach or vice versa at a given time is sub optimal, as both objectives can be targeted simultaneously with success.

It is evident that there are no other macro-level studies on MFIs in Sri Lanka in relation to the topic that this book deals with. In this context, this book resulted from an arduous task of updating and revising the doctoral thesis of the author could be a useful reference for microfinance practitioners, policy makers as well as undergraduate and graduate level students who study microfinance. The author's academic knowledge and his wealth of experience as a banker who has devoted more than thirty years of his professional life in dealing with the subject of rural development, have greatly helped him in producing this very informative and analytical book on microfinance.

ACKNOWLEDGEMENTS

This book is a revised and updated version of the Ph.D. thesis that I submitted to the Faculty of Graduate Studies, the University of Colombo in 2016. I am deeply grateful to everyone who has helped, supported and inspired me in the completion of the original thesis as well as this book.

I am indebted to my thesis supervisor, Dr. S M P Senanayake, former Professor of Economics, the University of Colombo for his support, advice and patience throughout this entire journey. I am grateful to him for helping me embark on a research that relates to the ongoing debates in the field of microfinance. He has been a source of great encouragement and guidance, and has been instrumental in improving the thesis substantially, with recommendation for its final submission. Words are just powerless to convey my sincere gratitude to him for his mature understanding and supervision along the way.

I am grateful to the pre-examiners for their insightful comments on my thesis. Important suggestions made by Dr. S P Premaratne from the University of Colombo, at various levels of the research and Prof. S S Colombage at the pre-submission stage of the thesis were very useful in the successful completion of the thesis.

Additionally, the help and support extended by the academic and other staff members of the Faculty of Graduate Studies, the University of Colombo, is greatly acknowledged and I am thankful to them. In particular, I wish to extend my gratitude to Dr. Ramani Gunathilake, from the University of Colombo, for her valuable feedback at the initial stage of the research and the PhD course coordinator of the Faculty of Graduate Studies, University of Colombo, Dr. Maringa Sumanadasa, for inspiring and encouraging me to finish the research on time. I also wish to thank Prof. Sunil Chandrasiri, and Prof. Nayani Melegoda, the former Dean and the present Dean of the Faculty of Graduate Studies, the University of

Colombo, respectively, for their guidance and advice on my research and academic life in general. Last but not least, I would like to thank Rev. Prof. W Wimalaratana Thero, and Prof. H D Karunaratne from the University of Colombo, for examining the thesis and recommending to award the degree of Doctor of Philosophy.

All this effort would not have been successful, if my wife Ayesha had not been so kind to me or cared for our two children, Chanulya and Ranmika with the love and affection due from both parents. They have been my pillars of strength, my greatest source of support and encouragement that makes life more meaningful and I hope they expect nothing from me but love and affection in return.

H Amarathunga
41/K, Nagenahira Mawatha
Kirillawala
Kadawatha
Sri Lanka

LIST OF ABREVIATIONS

ADB	Asian Development Bank
ANOVA	Analysis of Variance
ASPI	All Share Price Index
ATMs	Automated Teller Machines
BOC	Bank of Ceylon
CBSL	Central Bank of Sri Lanka
CFS	Consumer Finance and Socio-economic Survey
CP	Commercial Paper
CRBs	Co-operative Rural Banks
DCD	Department of Co-operative Development
DCS	Department of Census and Statistics
DSNBFIs	Department of Supervision of Non-Bank Financial Institutions
EFTPOS	Electronic Fund Transfer Facilities at Point of Sale Machines
EPF	Employees' Provident Fund
FTZs	Free Trade Zones
GDP	Gross Domestic Product
GLSs	Group Lending Schemes
IFS	International Financial Statistics
LKR	Sri Lankan Rupee

LMFPA	Lanka Microfinance Practitioners' Association
MBB	MicroBanking Bulletin
MFIs	Microfinance Institutions
(MIX) Market	Microfinance Information eXchange (MIX) Market
MLCF	Medium and Long Term Credit Fund
MPI	Milanka Price Index
NBFIs	Non-Bank Financial Institutions
NDB	National Development Bank
NDTF	National Development Trust Fund
NGOs	Non-Governmental Organizations
NTB	Nations Trust Bank
OSS	Operational Self-Sufficiency
HDI	Human Development Index
HIES	Household Income and Expenditure Surveys
HNB	Hatton National Bank
PB	People's Bank
PCI	Per Capita Income
PHC	Poverty Head Count
RO	Regional Office
PSB	Pradeshiya Sanwardana Bank
PTCCSs	SANASA Primary Thrift and Credit Co-operative Societies

RDB	Regional Development Bank
RFCs	Registered Finance Companies
RRDBs	Regional Rural Development Banks
RTGS	The Real Time Gross Settlement System
TCCSs	Thrift and Credit Co-operative Societies
SBSs	*Samurdhi* Bank Societies
SDBL	Sanasa Development Bank PLC
SFLCP-RF	Small Farmer and Landless Credit Project - Revolving Fund
SHGs	Self Help Groups
SLIPS	Sri Lanka Interbank Payment System
SMIB	State Mortgage and Investment Bank
USD	United States Dollar

CHAPTER 1

INTRODUCTION

MOTIVATION FOR THE STUDY

Microfinance has been regarded as one of the major tools to tackle poverty (Mersland and Strøm 2010; Robinson 2001; Rhyne 1998). Thus, researchers and policy makers have shown greater interest in studying microfinance operations in recent years. However, one of the most challenging issues that the microfinance institutions (MFIs) face today is how to design and implement their operations in order to achieve the objective of poverty reduction in a sustainable manner. For instance, if there is a tendency by MFIs to depend on wealthier customers to maintain financial sustainability, this focus may lead to a mission drift at the expense of outreach as emphasized by the welfarists.

In the light of growing concerns about the effectiveness of MFIs in reducing poverty, researchers have paid attention to studying the possible trade-off that might exist between poverty outreach and sustainability of MFIs (Quayes 2012; Hermes, Lensink and Meesters 2011; Mersland and Strøm 2010; Weiss and Montgomery 2005; Schreiner 2002; Robinson 2001; Morduch 2000). Empirical evidence also shows that MFIs have devised certain innovative means such as joint liability group lending schemes (GLSs)[1], to avoid a possible trade-off between the financial sustainability and outreach of microfinance programs (Hermes and Lensink 2007).

---

[1] Joint liability GLSs are a mechanism through which loans may be granted to members formed as a group, who usually possess a similar socio-economic background, and come from a same geographical area such as a village. Generally, under the GLSs, the collateral requirement of a loan by any member of the group is jointly shared among all members.

Sri Lanka has a variety of institutions falling under the category of MFIs. These institutions are considered to be distinctive from other formal financial institutions, mainly depending on the nature of clientele served by each group of institutions, and the lending methods adopted by them. Nevertheless, there are no uniquely common internal operations relevant to MFIs in reaching the poor. Certain differences in internal operations can be directly linked to policies of implementing programs relevant to poverty reduction and/or financial sustainability.

Even though, several studies have been carried out to assess the impact of MFIs on the poverty reduction of the country (Charitonenko and De Silva 2002; Shaw 2004; Tilakaratna, Wickramasinghe, and Kumara 2005), Sri Lanka is lagging behind in studies on the depth on poverty outreach in relation to the operations of MFIs in terms of their respective mandates. In particular, no macro-level study is available to assess the financial sustainability versus poverty outreach in the context of MFIs' operations in Sri Lanka.

The above context relating to microfinance in Sri Lanka has inspired me to undertake this study, which attempts to relate the ongoing debate on microfinance; if poverty outreach and sustainability are compatible or competing variables and whether lending methods adopted by MFIs make any differential impact on their outreach/sustainability, according to the Sri Lankan experience in microfinance.

PROBLEM AND ITS SETTING

Background

Outreach spreads into several dimensions, such as the breadth of outreach, depth of outreach, length of outreach and the scope of outreach (Schreiner 2002, 2). In general, focusing of any aspects of outreach may at least potentially, conflict with the financial sustainability of MFIs, as it is a costly affair to extend credit to the poor (Assefa, Hermes, and Meesters 2013). This view reflects the inherent nature of rural credit markets in developing countries where the requirement to grant many smaller size loans without collateral, to a larger number of poor customers mostly living in remote places has become commonplace.

The transaction costs of loans/savings of many financial institutions in developing countries represent a large fixed cost component and therefore the unit costs of smaller size loans/ savings to their associated risk/returns are higher in comparison with those of larger financial transactions to their associated risk/ returns (law of decreasing unit transaction costs with larger size transactions). Besides, there is also a default risk emanating from the lack of creditworthiness of the poor, mainly because of the absence of collateral, managerial and entrepreneurial capacity by them although according to Robinson (2001) many borrowers below the poverty line are creditworthy, while many above the line are not. Despite the rapid growth and operations based on group loans, dynamic incentives and frequent repayment, nearly half of the MFIs in the world have not returned a profit and depended on donors and subsidies (Sengupta and Aubuchon 2008, 22). In this context, achieving financial viability while reaching the poor effectively has become a challenging task for many MFIs operating in developing countries.

Some of the difficulties faced by MFIs in servicing the poor in developing countries could be a result of asymmetric information which relates to the problems of moral hazard and adverse selection (largely known as agency problems). Under the agency theory relating to credit markets, it is assumed that lenders are less informed of the borrowers' characteristics and riskiness of the projects that the borrowers intend to undertake.

When donor funding to certain MFIs gets diminished over time, such MFIs might want to transform their operations to be in line with commercial principles. This change could be visible in many fronts; switching to up market customers and economically active poor, entertaining larger size loans and diversifying the operations into lucrative areas of banking such as insurance and project consultancy. On the other hand, MFIs have also devised certain innovative means to reach the unreached poor effectively (Collins et al. 2009). However, the tendency to transform operations based entirely on commercial principles has raised doubt on the MFIs success in poverty outreach, the real mandate that they are supposed to accomplish.

Existing literature shows that there are two competing camps of microfinance operational models. The proponents of the welfarist view believe that small enterprises cannot sustain and proceed with market rates payable on their borrowings from profit oriented MFIs and thus the poorest of the poor cannot be served by such MFIs. The institutionalists however claim that credit facilities available at below market rates in developing countries would more often lead to malpractices such as the delivery of credit to better-off, at the expense of the poor. Further, the staff of MFIs may opt to give loans to people whom they like, an approach depicting clear case of moral hazard on the part of MFIs (Hudon and Traca 2011). The institutionalists also claim that the cost relating to the administration of MFIs is high so that such costs should be covered through the adoption of prudential banking norms. Financial sustainability, thus, makes it easier for them to penetrate into the very poor clients. Besides, institutionalists also affirm that MFIs can earn operational efficiency when employees actively contribute towards high productivity and recovery of loans. Therefore, according to the proponents of institutionalists, financial efficiency reflects sound policies on the internal operations of MFIs.

Sri Lanka has a variety of MFIs such as Pradeshiya Sanwardhana Bank/ Regional Development Bank (PSB/RDB)[2], Licensed Commercial/Specialized Banks (LCBs, LSBs), SANASA

---

[2] Pradeshiya Sanwardana Bank was established on July 14, 2010, by amalgamating Regional Development Banks.

Development Bank PLC (SDBL), Co-operative Rural Banks (CRBs) and other co-operatives such as Women's Development Co-operatives, Thrift and Credit Co-operative Societies (TCCSs), *Samurdhi* Bank Societies (SBSs), Non-Governmental Organizations (NGOs), Limited Liability Companies/Companies Limited by Guarantee and other financial institutions such as finance companies.[3]

Only a few providers of microfinance in Sri Lanka come under different regulatory and supervisory mechanisms. SBSs are regulated by the *Samurdhi* Authority of Sri Lanka while the CRBs and TCCSs are regulated by the Department of Co-operative Development (DCD). The RDBs and other licensed banks, fall under the purview of the Central Bank of Sri Lanka (CBSL). A large number of other NGOs involved in microfinance do not fall under any kind of external supervisory authority.[4] In the context of current status quo on MFI regulation, this study pays no attention to analyze regulatory aspects on the depth of outreach.

Statement of the Problem

Microfinance has evolved since 1990s as a strategy that supports the poor people who fall outside the formal financial system, to engage themselves in income generating activities thereby helping them to

---

[3] The number of outlets of these institutions had been estimated to be around 10000 in 2010 according to GTZ - ProMiS (promotion of the microfinance sector). GTZ - ProMiS is a programme implemented by Ministry of Finance and Planning of Sri Lanka in partnership with the German Technical Cooperation (GTZ) on behalf of the German Federal Ministry for Economic Cooperation and Development (BMZ).

[4] The Microfinance Act, No. 6 of 2016 provides for the registration of NGO MFIs registered under the Voluntary Social Services Organizations (Registration and Supervision) Act, No. 31 of 1980 (VSSO Act), by the registrar of voluntary social service organizations. However, currently there is no sound supervisory mechanism in place to supervise MFIs apart from the requirement for registration under the said Act.

leave out of poverty. Accordingly, microfinance has become a powerful tool to fight against poverty (World Bank, 2006). However, under the changing market conditions and situation of the poor, empirical evidence shows that MFIs are encountering greater challenges in accomplishing their mission, and paradigm changes in their operations are taking place. Hermes, Lensink and Meesters (2011, 938) summarize these challenges into the following five areas; i) increased competition among MFIs, ii) entry of commercial banks in providing microfinance, iii) interest of large investors worldwide to finance MFIs, iv) emergence of new banking technology and v) liberalization of financial markets by developing countries. Looking through studies which focus on these issues and challenges, the operations of MFIs could be classified into three heterogeneous groups which may however not be exhaustive.

i. MFIs which focus on poverty outreach but face challenges in maintaining sustainability
ii. MFIs which focus on sustainability but face challenges in reaching the poor
iii. MFIs which focus on sustainability and poverty outreach simultaneously, and meet the challenges effectively

Although the empirical evidence and theoretical explanations show high cost involved in MFIs operations, as a matter of fact, MFIs have to address wider social goals, and thus need to lend small loans to very poor borrowers at a low cost (Mersland and Strøm 2010). The social mission of this nature is part and partial of poverty focused approach of MFIs which are expected to make available financial services to the poor at subsidized rates while sometimes depending themselves on subsidized funds and grants.

There are however, widespread doubts regarding the fact that MFIs focus on poverty makes them sustainable institutions. Therefore, arguably as a rational entity, MFIs may change the focus in the pursuit of profit, to individual-based lending, larger sized loans, economically active poor and lending at market rates. Understandably, less profitability would mean MFIs are less sustainable, and face a risk of encountering a mission failure. Conversely, running MFIs based on a profit motivation drive would lead to achieve sustainability at the expense of a mission drift.

On the debate of trade-off between sustainability and outreach, the welfarist view stresses the importance of outreach and the threat of focusing too much on sustainability, while the institutionalists claim that MFIs should focus on sustainability and efficiency (Hermes, Lensink and Meesters 2011). In other words, as far as their operations are concerned, MFIs face a challenge as to which approach to be followed, i.e., to pursue more profitability at the cost of outreach or more outreach at the cost of sustainability. When the transformation of operations of MFIs to achieve sustainability from an existing poverty focused approach is a gradual process, MFIs may have enough space and time to mitigate any possible mission drifts with the adoption of novel microfinance models. Such MFIs would be able to manage both sustainability and outreach in a successful manner.

Key Questions Raised

MFIs that are grouped into three areas as indicated earlier, underpinned core issues that need to be analyzed with regard to operations of MFIs in Sri Lanka. Accordingly, we make effort to find out answers to following specific questions in this study.

a) Do MFIs in Sri Lanka successfully achieve financial sustainability in relation to depth of poverty outreach?

Currently, MFIs in Sri Lanka implement different types of lending schemes. As the cost and efficiency of each MFI would vary, it is assumed that the difference in financial sustainability versus poverty outreach could also be explained by the types of lending methods adopted by each MFI.

In this backdrop, this study attempts to seek answers to the following question.

b) Do the different lending methods adopted by MFIs in Sri Lanka affect their sustainability and/or depth of poverty outreach?

This study also focuses attention on some additional key questions as follows.

c) Does the operational self-sufficiency (OSS) of MFIs affect their achievement of poverty outreach?
d) Does the volume of assets/loans of MFIs affect their achievement of poverty outreach?
e) What impact does the employment of female loan officers by MFIs have on MFIs' achievement of poverty outreach?
f) What impact does the increase of number of branches by MFIs have on MFIs' achievement of poverty outreach?

Objectives of the Study

The main objective of this study is to;

a) examine the possible trade-off (or compatibility) between sustainability and poverty outreach of MFIs in Sri Lanka.

The other specific objectives of the study are to;

b) identify the key variables that affect poverty outreach by MFIs in Sri Lanka
c) investigate the lending methods adopted by MFIs in Sri Lanka on the MFIs' financial sustainability and

d) provide insight into the formulation of an effective operational framework for MFIs in Sri Lanka to achieve financial sustainability versus poverty outreach.

Limitation of the Study

One of the major limitations of a study on microfinance operations in Sri Lanka is the lack of continuous data for a considerable period to conduct certain statistical analyses. Hence, the author took measures to collect data from different secondary sources and MFIs themselves which are under review, by paying attention to maintain uniformity and consistency of data collected.

SIGNIFICANCE OF THE STUDY

Considering the fact that poverty levels record significant differences at provincial and district levels in Sri Lanka and the poor people who are yet unreached by financial institutions might be the most economically vulnerable group of the country, it can be assumed that there is a greater importance of understanding the link between financial sustainability and poverty outreach of MFIs in Sri Lanka.

Significance to Microfinance Literature

This study captures country-specific factors in depth such as market conditions, institutional environment, and a variety of other social and cultural factors in analyzing operations of MFIs. Therefore, a reader can grasp new insights in understanding microfinance operations in Sri Lanka, especially on whether actions of MFIs have led to a mission drift or not.

The sample consisting of 50 MFIs operating in Sri Lanka represents 85 percent of client outreach, 54 percent of lending portfolio and 39 percent of deposit portfolio of MFIs in the country was thoroughly researched in this study. Therefore, the book stands out as a comprehensive investigation of MFI activities of Sri Lanka with macro-level perspective and enriches the existing microfinance literature as the findings would be conclusive and strong.

Significance to the Theoretical Work

The problem of asymmetric information prevailing in credit markets where the poor are abundantly present is complex. Obviously, it is the financial institutions that have to grapple with issues such as the lack of credit histories and collateral of the potential customers. The financial institutions face the difficulty in observing the differences in credit quality among borrowers in the absence of their credit histories. This results in inefficiency in credit markets. As a result, application of high interest rates and credit rationing has become part of the business to mitigate adverse selection. Armendariz and Morduch (2011) maintain that lenders are faced with the problem of observing the efforts being made by the borrower or the realization of project returns which are called ex-ante and ex-post moral hazard respectively.

As described in the theory on microfinance, MFIs design appropriate strategies to address the problems of adverse selection and moral hazard existing in credit markets. For instance, the joint liability schemes are successfully adopted by MFIs world over as a way of overcoming the requirement to provide collateral by borrowers. Some MFIs in Sri Lanka adopt the joint responsibility concept, particularly by forming homogenous groups of poor prior to the granting of loans to them. This study will examine the impact of microfinance lending models on the efficiency and outreach of MFIs, and therefore, the applications of theoretical explanation on credit markets where the poor carry out their transactions, could be further verified through the empirical evidence emanating from this study.

STRUCTURE OF THE BOOK

The book consists of six chapters. The introductory chapter focuses on explaining the motivation for the book, problem and its setting including the objectives, expected contribution and limitations of the study. The second chapter reviews the theoretical and empirical literature on microfinance particularly in relation to the sustainability and poverty outreach of MFIs. In this chapter, several key areas of related literature, namely supply leading finance, interest rate dilemma, strategic options, the asymmetric information paradigm, informal credit markets, savings of the poor and the mission drift in microfinance have been reviewed. Chapter three examines the historical evolution of MFIs in Sri Lanka in relation to the macroeconomic and financial environment including the poverty aspects of the country. A brief discussion on analytical framework of the study is presented in the fourth chapter, while the fifth chapter is devoted to the analysis of data and the description of the research findings. Chapter six presents general conclusions of the research along with some recommendations on microfinance policy formulation and further microfinance research studies that may be carried out in the future.

CHAPTER 2

REVIEW OF MICROFINANCE LITERATURE

INTRODUCTION

MFIs have been operating with different degrees of impact on many facets of people's livelihood in developing countries. MFIs today adopt various operational methodologies under the broader context of poverty lending approach or financial systems approach to achieve their objectives. In this backdrop, this chapter provides a detailed description of the theoretical and empirical explanations of the main issues of microfinance that relate to the topic of the book.

Theories relating to microfinance could be explainable in the context of providing finance to the poor through the rural credit and other micro lending programs. The history of rural credit programs is relatively long although the term 'microfinance' has emerged in the mainstreams of economics and banking only during last three or four decades.[5] Thus, microfinance would have begun in conjunction with or following some massive programs of rural credit, mostly subsidized ones which were implemented by developing countries during the 1970s and 1980s to assist poor households. Although, these rural credit programs comprised of loans targeted to the poor at low rates of interest, the effectiveness of the programs was not impressive due to many reasons, including the heavy involvements of the governments in the implementation of the programs. In this situation, microfinance became a new way of addressing the

---

[5] "The roots of microfinance can be found in many places, but the best known story is that of Muhammad Yunus and the founding of Bangladesh Grameen Bank during latter part of 1970s." (Armendariz and Morduch 2011).

problems of poverty of both rural and urban poor with the provision of finance and other credit-plus services to them.

In this chapter, theoretical concepts relevant to the theme of the book are discussed on the basis of the local finance theories explained by Robinson (2001) while the rest of the literature in this chapter provides a broader view of poverty lending approach versus financial systems approach. Accordingly, the chapter is developed under sub topics such as the different definitions available on microfinance and main features of MFIs, supply leading finance, the asymmetric information paradigm, informal credit markets, savings and the poor, the challenges in the provision of credit to low-income groups and the innovative mechanisms on risk sharing adopted by MFIs relating to the provision of credit to such low-income groups, the current debates of MFIs, mission drift in microfinance and the impact of regulations on the sustainability and poverty outreach of MFIs. The section before the summary of the chapter provides an overview of Sri Lankan literature on the subject of microfinance.

The study of theoretical views on microfinance helps the reader to understand the fundamentals on the emergence of microfinance while policy makers to grasp issues relating to rural development and poverty. Further, the lending institutions may be benefitted to make effective decisions in lending to the rural communities in developing countries.

DEFINITIONS AND MAIN FEATURES OF MFIs

Definitions

A detailed definition of microfinance has been presented by Robinson (2001, 9). Accordingly, microfinance is "small-scale financial services - primarily credit and savings provided to people who farm or fish or herd; who operate small enterprises or microenterprises where goods are produced, recycled, repaired, or sold; who provide services; who work for wages or commissions; who gain income from renting out small amount of land, vehicles, draft animals, or machinery and tools; and to other individuals and groups at the local levels of developing countries, both rural and urban." This definition encompasses a wide array of business activities that come under the microfinance sector and emphasize that MFIs should focus on extending small-scale financial services to entrepreneurs engaged in such activities. In developing countries, small-scale entrepreneurs face difficulties in accessing most of competitive financial services under favorable terms and conditions, necessitating financial institutions such as MFIs to address the said difficulties.

The term microfinance means "the provision of financial services (generally savings and credit) to low-income clients" (Ledgerwood 1999, 1). Further, the clients referred in this definition includes, traders, street vendors, small farmers, service providers (hairdressers, rickshaw drivers), and artisans and small producers, such as blacksmiths and seamstresses. It is stated that many such clients have a stable source of income since they engage in multiple sources of income generation activities. Therefore, the clients of MFIs, according to Ledgerwood (1999) are generally not considered to be the poorest of the poor but economically active poor, who could facilitate MFIs to achieve sustainability.

MFIs are broadly categorized as financial intuitions that have motivation to assist typically poor households and small-scale enterprises in getting access to financial services (Hardy, Holden and Prokopenko 2003). This definition reflects that there is a need to address the issue of poverty on a priority basis. The same line of thinking is shared by many other researchers who maintain that the prime objective of MFIs is to provide financial services to the poor in order for them to exit from poverty and improve their social and economic conditions on a sustainable basis (Mersland and Strøm 2010; Rhyne 1998; Robinson 2001). Further, as Karlan and Goldberg (2007, 3-4) explain "microfinance for loans (i.e., microcredit) is the provision of small-scale financial services to people who lack access to traditional banking services." According to them the features of microfinance consist of small transactions, loans for entrepreneurial activity, collateral-free loans, group lending, targeting poor clients, targeting female clients, simple application processes, provision of services in underserved communities, and market-level interest rates among other things.

The definitions of both the Asian Development Bank (ADB) and Microfinance Information eXchange (MIX) Market on microfinance are important in order to specifically understand the institutional view of microfinance. The ADB defines that microfinance as the provision of a broad range of financial services, such as deposits, loans, payment services, money transfers, and insurance, to poor and low-income households, and; their microenterprises (Asian Development Bank 2000). The MIX provides a functional definition of microfinance services, which are "as opposed to financial services in general - retail financial services that are relatively small in relation to the income of a typical individual. Specifically, the average outstanding balance of microfinance products is no greater than 250 percent of the average income per person (GNI per capita)."

In the literature on microfinance, it has been often found that the terms microcredit and microfinance are used interchangeably. However, an in depth understanding of the two terms show that they represent two distinctive areas of credit. Hulme (2000) points out that the emphasis placed by MFIs on microenterprise lending has resulted in the evolution of the microfinance industry. Microfinance involves offering of banking products and services on the basis of the needs of the poor and improving the saving habits of the poor through methods that are attractive to them. Microcredit is only a component of microfinance, which involves microcredit plus many other non-credit financial services.

With the understanding of these definitions, it can be assumed that clientele base of an MFI is typically the poor people of the society, who could be small-scale entrepreneurs with a low capacity to save and invest. The definitions generally, as expected, do not extend to include detailed operational aspects of microfinance or innovative and flexible lending and deposit schemes adopted by MFIs in reaching the poor. Definitions provide only a broader outline of the salient aspects of microfinance, particularly relevant to developing countries. However, in terms of the operational features and the approaches adopted in dealing with their customers, there can be significant differences among MFIs.

Main Features of MFIS

Despite the fact that the modalities of the provision of credit and mobilization of deposits differ from one MFI to another, there are common characteristics that can be identified among MFIs. These common characteristics need to be understood especially in the context of the theoretical underpinnings as well as their becoming a commonplace in the economics of microfinance.

i Reaching the poor

One of the greatest challenges of microfinance is to reach the poor and find ways and means for them to exit from poverty. The poor are usually caught up in a vicious circle of poverty which provides little room for them to pursue income generating activities unless they are financially supported. It is amidst this backdrop that poverty focused MFIs are supposed to play an important role in order to uplift the living conditions of the poor. There is widespread literature that affirms that the motivation for microfinance emanates as a methodology for alleviating poverty (Mersland and Strøm 2010; Brau and Woller 2004; Morduch 2000; Rhyne 1998). This justifies the emergence of microfinance on the global stage today.

MFIs are easily susceptible to serve clients who are creditworthy and economically viable because of the fact that profitability can be ensured easily through lending to such clients. The poor are also creditworthy when they are economically active even though they may encounter difficulties in offering outright collaterals against any intended loan facility. Targeting the poorest of the poor and financing their projects would not be financially viable. Targeting the poor, according to Conning (1999), bears higher staff costs and needs the application of higher interest rates, and such MFIs are poorly leveraged than those targeting less poor borrowers.

In the above contexts, it is expected that MFIs are generally willing to serve 'economically active poor' rather than the 'extreme poor'. Robinson (2001, 17-18) distinguishes the differences between these two terms and presents it in a nutshell as shown below.

> The poor may suffer from lack of food and water, unemployment or underemployment, disease, abuse, homelessness, degradation, and disenfranchisement. The result among those affected often include physical, mental, and emotional disability, limited skills and education, low self-esteem and lack of self-confidence, and fear, resentment, aggression, and truncated vision…"
> It is important to distinguish between extreme poor from economically active poor. "….extreme poverty exists below the minimum subsistence level; they include those who are unemployed or severely underemployed, as well as those whose work is so poorly remunerated that their purchasing power does not permit the minimum caloric intake required to overcome malnutrition." "The term economically active poor, in contrast, is used in a general sense to refer to those among the poor who have some form of employment, and who are not severely food-deficit or destitute.

There can be no direct role entrusted to MFIs in providing credit or any other services to the poor who are living without basic necessities such as food, shelter, education and health below basic minimum requirements. Usually, such problems of the poor people are left for the government in power to take necessary actions.

A broader conceptualization of targeting the poor can be shown in a schematic representation as given in Figure 1.

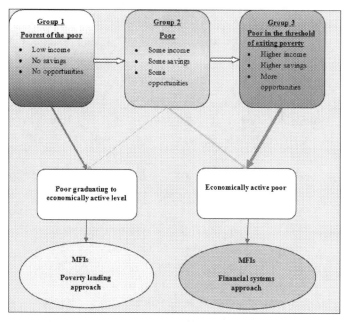

Figure 2.1 Targeting the Poor by MFIs
Source: By the Author

Figure 2.1 identifies three groups of poor who are in i. extreme poverty (group 1) ii. poverty (group 2) and iii the threshold of exiting poverty (group 3), based on the concept of income poverty. It is assumed under normal circumstances, the people in group 1 will attempt to shift to group 2 and people in group 2 will attempt to shift to group 3. MFIs which follow the financial systems approach are concerned with the economically active population from group 2 and group 3 and financial services are available to them, if they are considered to be creditworthy customers. Eventually, it is assumed that viable customers become small and medium scale entrepreneurs, who at that point onwards, need to be directed to maintain relationships with mainstream financial institutions. MFIs which adopt poverty lending approaches, are keen to cater to the poor in group1 and group 2. The poor in these two groups need to be upgraded to 'economically active poor' for meaningful poverty outreach and sustainability of the MFIs involved in the process. The involvement of MFIs in the provision of skills and other credit plus services to the poor is vital for upgrading the poor into 'economically active poor'.

The schematic representation reflects broadly the views expressed by Morduch (2000). Accordingly, it is described that microfinance programs encompasses various activities which focus on providing financial support to the poor and this common attitude and pursuance is reflected under the financial systems approach as well as poverty lending approach. Although many people consider that the provision of microfinance to tackle the issue of vicious circle of poverty as a major breakthrough, those food-deficit extreme poor cannot be served through microfinance in the same way as the economically active poor are assisted. Overall, servicing of extreme poor remains a costly affair for MFIs, especially if the MFIs do not increase efficiency to match their increasing costs.

ii Group lending methodology

Group lending is a methodology in which the responsibility of sharing the risk associated with any loan granted is passed to the entire members of the group. In commercial credit markets, the banks establish the creditworthiness of the borrowers and demand collateral to cover the risk, aspects of which are considered of little use in micro credit markets. In view of this, MFIs have introduced the widely accepted peer pressure system normally associated with group lending, in order to succeed in monitoring the use of loans and repayment of the borrowers. Thus, the GLSs have emerged as a way of meeting the problems of information asymmetry successfully. Eventually, group lending has evolved as a viable mechanism of extending institutional credit to poor people, whose main problem of getting access to credit has been the lack of creditworthiness, resulting from issues of collateral, entrepreneurial capabilities, marketing of products etc. All these issues may not be addressed successfully through the implementation of GLSs, but it can at least replace the conventional assets based collateral with some form of social collateral.

The risk sharing mechanism under GLSs is often criticized for its failure to encourage the people to save (De Laiglesia 2006). Correa and Correa (2009) mention that joint liability models are an illustration of the poverty lending approach whose thrust is subsidies. Tassel (1999), demonstrates in a theoretical paper, that the joint liability can ease the lender to identify heterogeneous borrower types as the borrowers have better information on each other's risks. MFIs can thus encourage low-risk borrowers to group with one another and seek group loans at low interest rates while facilitating high-risk borrowers to seek individual loans at somewhat higher interest rates. Ghatak (2002) has also argued that group lending can solve the problem of lenders, as risky and safe borrowers group into one which is homogenous to each other.

However, positive assortative matching does not necessarily hold true if the lending is extended to incorporate the dynamic incentives as suggested by Guttman (2008). Using two types of borrowers, risky type and safe type, Guttman (2008) shows theoretically that the safe borrower is willing to pay more, in order to have another safe borrower as his partner rather than a risky borrower. Under these circumstances, in the group formation, risky borrowers and safe borrowers form groups separately. It is therefore assumed only as a special case where the positive assortative matching does not hold true when dynamic incentives are associated with group lending. Morduch (2000) shows that there is a tendency to group similar risk types together when joint liability is accompanied by additional incentives. Usually, in group loan contracts, joint liability makes each member of the group mutually liable for the members' repayment. Tassel (1999) has developed a theoretical paper focusing on the role of joint liability and demonstrates that lenders can utilize joint liability to screen borrowers, as the low-risk borrowers group with one another while high-risk borrowers select individual loans at higher interest rates.

MFIs could achieve a drastic reduction in monitoring the clients' use of credit under a proper formation of groups. This fact has been affirmed by Cason, Gangadharan and Maitra (2012) who have examined the lending, monitoring and repayment behavior in groups and individual lending schemes using experimental methods. They report that group lending leads to higher monitoring and improved repayment rates, provided that the peer monitoring is less costly than lender monitoring. Meanwhile, Godquin (2004) having conducted a research on microfinance repayment performance in Bangladesh, concludes that group homogeneity is not found to affect the repayment performance in a significant way but the nonfinancial services extended to group members have a better impact on repayment.

iii Dynamic incentives

The case of Grameen Bank shows that group methodology is employed usefully but certain conditions such as community specific reasons have made the scheme vulnerable and less effective in countering the problem of information asymmetry. Thus, some forms of dynamic incentives have been introduced lately, as the concept of group lending cannot be employed on all occasions of operations in microfinance. The dynamic incentives are usually operated as supplements to group lending.

Dynamic incentives are elaborated through the repeated interaction between borrower and lender. For instance, borrowers can be cautioned with a threat of not providing further loans if they fail to repay on time, or conversely, they are guaranteed with larger loans in the next 'loan cycle' if the current loans are repaid promptly. Rewarding the borrower with a larger loan for his good conduct of repayment is called progressive lending, which assures the persistent delivery of microfinance services to the borrower. Naveen Kumar (2012), having conducted a primary survey of 106 self help groups (SHGs) in Karnataka, India, affirms that progressive lending has contributed towards the improvement of loan sizes across the groups and regions. In contrast, those borrowers who are defaulted may also be reported to an independent body which could in turn disseminate such information among lending banks, creating an adverse impact on the borrowers so reported.

The lenders are able to identify borrowers' reaction at the beginning of the processing of the loan if dynamic incentives are in place. Lenders are thus able to assess the repayment capacity of a borrower to some extent at the initial stages of the granting of a loan. On the other hand, borrowers are also induced to fulfill their obligation of repayment on time through dynamic incentives. However, the presence of a large number of players of MFIs in the loan markets in developing countries, and/or news on impending failures of MFIs could function against the success achievable through dynamic incentives.

Dynamic incentives are a powerful instrument that can improve the financial condition of MFIs on a long-term basis. For instance, Tedeschi (2006) shows that with the use of dynamic incentives, microfinance could become a sustainable development alternative, particularly in markets where outreach is less costly and market players are less risky. The same research further indicates that if the borrowers can be protected from expenditure and income vulnerabilities and assured of meeting the economic loss if it happens with some form of confidence, the borrowers' ability to repay could increase.

Use of dynamic incentives becomes less effective when the same incentive is applied on the borrower for a considerable period of time without researching the change of interest of the borrower on such incentives. Granting of larger loans to borrowers could be inefficient as the age of their borrowing group increases and it is therefore suggested that new incentives be developed for experienced borrowers for the purpose of maintaining good repayment rates (Godquin 2004). Innovative incentives, such as the granting of higher interest on the deposit of the borrower or charging lower interest on the amount of borrower's loans, could be useful in achieving higher repayment rates in microfinance.

iv Frequent repayment of installments

The frequent repayment of the installments of loans is assumed to reduce the delinquency ratio of lending institutions. Unlike in established markets where lenders collect loan repayment on the basis of income generation of the projects for which the loan is granted, MFIs usually adopt a repayment policy, requiring the borrowers to pay the installments after a few weeks of the grant of loans. The frequent collection of money from small borrowers and constant monitoring not only impose some kind of financial discipline on borrowers to meet their obligation, but it also helps them to improve their savings habits and interactions with formal financial institutions. Jane and Mansuri (2003) argue that the rigid installment plan enables MFIs to make use of the monitoring ability possessed by the informal lender in constraining the strategic behavior of the borrower. Owing to repayment, which falls immediately after the loan disbursement, or even before project returns are realized, MFIs could ensure that moral hazard behavior on the part of the borrower is curtailed. It is viewed that frequent repayment, as a response to the information asymmetric problem, can be explainable as a method of inculcating fiscal discipline among borrowers.

Even though, the financial discipline imposed by frequent repayment is critical in preventing default, economic theory suggests that flexible repayment schedules are useful for clients to improve their loan repayment. This proposition, supported by the economic theory, is further confirmed by Field and Pande (2008), with a conduct of a field experiment. They argue that client delinquency or default has no significant impact by weekly or monthly repayment schedules and suggest that a more flexible schedule can significantly lower the cost of transactions without increasing the defaults of clients.

v Targeting women

MFIs should be willing to target female clientele more than male clientele for several well-known reasons commonly discussed within the microfinance industry. Firstly, women are easily susceptible to the peer pressure which is needed for lenders to achieve better repayment rates. Secondly, poverty defined in terms of criteria, such as the level of children's education and health, can be meaningfully addressed when women are empowered and given opportunities to rise against the vicious circle of poverty they are engulfed in without any rationale. Thirdly, women are supposed to be more responsive than males to the lenders' call to report the progress of their projects. Fourthly, the loans granted to female clients are comparatively smaller in size corresponding with the poverty outreach target of MFIs as against commercially oriented MFIs which have a decreasing portion of their lending to women clients. Accessing capital and its use can be identified and differentiated by women versus men according to Premaratne (2002).

There has been empirical evidence to show that women are capable of bringing about more impact on family welfare than their male counterparts if they are given opportunities to control more resources (Breierova and Duflo 2004). This proposition could be mostly applicable to developing countries where women are often assigned the task of looking after their children. A theoretical model developed by Ngo and Wahhaj (2011) has identified that women borrowers can benefit more in comparison to male borrowers, when they invest loans profitability in joint activity. D'espallier, Gue'rin and Mersland (2011), by studying 350 MFIs in 70 countries, have found that female clients are associated with lower portfolio risk and fewer portfolio write-offs. Interestingly, according to them, MFIs need to make less provision when they have a higher proportion of female clients. This research further highlights that NGOs, individual-based lenders, and regulated MFIs are benefitted more from focusing on women.

vi High administrative costs

The transaction costs of a loan have a large fixed cost component so that the ratio of costs to smaller sized loans are higher in comparison with that of larger sized loans. The law of decreasing unit transaction costs with the increase in the size of transactions is a known phenomenon in credit markets. Hence, MFIs would also be susceptible to acquire cost efficiency with the grant of larger loans. However, as argued by Armendariz and Szafarz (2009), MFIs possess larger average loan sizes not because they could minimize the transaction cost but also due to some other factors such as interplay between their own mission and region-specific clientele parameters.

If MFIs are required to raise funds at certain costs, it is prudent for them to cover this cost through the income generated from lending and other investments. Since other investment opportunities available to an MFI are limited, the cost of funds on deposits mobilized by many MFIs have to be covered through the interest income charged on loans granted. However, MFIs have to meet comparatively high costs relative to the grant of loans for the purpose of screening borrowers, following-up projects, maintaining documents and the payment of salaries to the staff. The probability of having high delinquency ratios of loans requires these institutions to allocate significant amount of provision. Overall, the administrative costs per loans are expected to rise, corresponding to the level of involvement by MFIs in servicing small loans relative to the servicing of big loans. Hermes, Lensink and Meesters (2011) having studied 435 MFIs show that the trend of increasing cost of transactions of very small loans is due to the screening, monitoring and administration of loans.

The poor are generally willing to accept credit under subsidized rates, although the effectiveness of such credit for the poor to exit from poverty has come under some criticism. There are arguments that the application of relatively high interest rates by MFIs, in comparison to the capacity of the poor to meet such costs, would eventually lead to the improvement of the income generating capacity of the poor. In this context, the higher interest rates of MFIs, resulting from rising administrative costs indirectly become an inducement for micro entrepreneurs to perform efficiently. This view is implicitly supported by Cull, Demirguc-Kunt and Morduch (2011) who argue that MFIs, in order to cover rising costs, need to increase the rate of interest for the loans granted with the assurance of high returns to the capital on those projects so assisted.

RURAL FINANCE IN RELATION TO SUPPLY LEADING HYPOTHESIS

Conceptual Reasoning

Supply leading finance refers to a situation where financial facilities are provided to a certain industry or entrepreneurs in advance of the demand for the same in order to spur the economic growth (Levine 1997). In this context, as far as rural credit markets are concerned, the provision of credit to the poor households should affect the increase in their level of income. A large and diverse body of theoretical and empirical literature has discussed the relationship between financial development and economic growth. Much earlier work on this subject can even be traced as far back as to Bagehot (1873), which described how the industrialization of England was facilitated by the availability of a large amount of money for 'immense works'.

The supply leading hypothesis prescribes that the deliberate creation of financial institutions and markets are essential in order to increase real growth while the most competing view, demand following hypothesis postulates that only economic growth creates demand for more financial services and as a result the financial systems will grow only in response to such economic expansions. The point of view of the latter case is that increased economic activities will result in more demand for both physical and liquid capital. In this context, the growth in the real sector induces the financial sector to expand, and thereby increases the competition and efficiency of financial intermediaries and markets.

Savings mobilization from rural households in many developing countries has been comparatively low in comparison with rest of the economy. Therefore, in the event of a big demand for credit by rural communities, financial institutions would seek out funds from other sources or else ration the credit. Commercial banks, also adopt a stringent approach in lending to the poor as poor are unable to meet many requirements of banks for such lending. In this backdrop, subsidized credits, often available through government sponsored programs had been very popular in developing countries since 1960s.

Financial Repression Versus Financial Liberalization

The subject of financial repression versus financial liberalization comes as an essential part under the broader concept of supply leading theory. The views of McKinnon (1973) and Shaw (1973), which are referred to as the 'McKinnon–Shaw' hypothesis, emerged as a leading theoretical presentation on the positive effect of financial development on growth in the 1970s. According to this hypothesis, inflation, interest rate ceilings and subsidization, heavy reserve requirements on bank deposits, and compulsory credit allocations are unattractive for the development of a domestic banking system. These controls are present in a repressed system which often shows negative real rates of interest on monetary assets, resulting in a fall in demand for money against the GDP.

Financial repression, in the context of the 'McKinnon–Shaw' hypothesis, would hint that the savers in developing countries should be cautious in protecting their wealth and consider reducing the flow of savings through the banking sector. Thus, the availability of loanable funds for investment would be curtailed and the process of banking development would be impeded thereby lowering the rate of economic growth. Investors find it difficult to obtain funds as people tend to invest in instruments that hedge against inflation.

The policy recommendation of 'McKinnon–Shaw' to achieve growth is that prices should be stabilized through relevant macroeconomic policy, and positive real rates of interest need to be achieved through the removal of controls and restrictions on the banking sector. In other words, financial liberalization is necessary for the development of the financial sector and the growth of the economy. A large number of theoretical and empirical studies have supported the view that there is a positive relationship between financial development and growth (Caldero'n and Liu 2003; Ahmed and Ansari 1998; Odedokun 1996; King and Levine 1993a).

The acceptance of the one-way causality from financial development to growth has been questioned by some economists, asserting that financial development follows the development of an economy (demand following hypothesis) and not vice versa. Robinson (1952) who pioneered this view stressed the fact that "where enterprise leads finance follows." On the contrary, Lucas (1988) argues that financial factors can play a little role in the process of growth declaring that "economists badly over-stress the role of financial factors in economic growth". The examination of the causal relationship between finance and economic growth relating to Sri Lanka shows that financial development follows economic growth (Amarathunga 2008).

Do the Poor Deserve Financial Facilities?

The 'McKinnon–Shaw' hypothesis, which prescribes that financial liberalization leads to the efficient allocation of resources, was not appealing enough to policy makers in developing countries. Thus, government intervention is prominent in the allocation of resources to targeted areas and sectors in most developing countries. For instance, Stiglitz (1994) mentions that financial repression in developing countries does not curtail growth, as the mechanism for resource allocation in these countries is impaired due to market failures[6] requiring government intervention imperative in the resource allocation process (this does not necessarily mean that directed credit is a solution). Further, cheap credit to the poor in many developing countries is justified for many other reasons, including the problems of access to credit, scarcity of funds especially long-term finance, and inability of informal sector (representing money lenders, pawn brokers, local traders etc.) to meet the demand for credit at reasonable rates of interest.

Interest rate, as the price of credit, is determined competitively based on supply and demand conditions, when there are no market failures. This means that *Pareto efficiency*[7] prevails in competitive credit markets. Experiences of developing countries confirm that financial markets fail in mobilizing and allocating resources in a socially optimal way. Thus, the governments in developing countries are compelled to intervene in the market and channel credit to targeted purposes and people at subsidized rates. Hence, it is expected that positive externalities would emerge from the

---

[6] Market failures in relation to the credit market, refer to the inability of competitive market forces to allocate credit efficiently among economic units. For instance, loans to certain prospective borrowers cannot be extended due to lack of collateral possessed by them.

[7] *Pareto efficiency*, in a nutshell is a state of economic allocation of resources in which it is impossible to make any one further better off without making at least one individual worse off.

grant of subsidized credit, which are necessary for achieving two main objectives, namely economic efficiency and the equitable distribution of the income.

a Economic efficiency argument

In most of the developing countries, people in low income categories are engaged in producing primary goods and services, involving agriculture. The low income of these people is often attributed to their incapacity/unwillingness to adopt new technologies that would bring about cost efficiency and productivity. The poor have been deprived of accessing capital required to engage in such modernization. This is a vicious circle that the poor are caught up in and, therefore, providing finance is an essential ingredient in disentangling the whole process.

It is the government which has to intervene in the first place to provide necessary finances to small-scale entrepreneurs who may also after receiving funds, shift from the use of labor intensive techniques to capital intensive techniques. Economic efficiency is expected to be achieved through productivity increase and cost efficiency, against a situation where commercial banks are not ready to fund low-income entrepreneurs for the modernization of their enterprises. Under these circumstances, subsidizing the capital cost of projects through low interest credit is justified based on the positive externalities expected through such projects.

b Income distribution argument

Low income, low investment, and low savings are the key elements of a so called 'vicious circle' preventing the poor from accumulating assets. In these circumstances, the poor do not have the capacity for investments or savings as the income they receive is not sufficient even for their basic consumption requirements.

On the other hand, commercial banks are viewed as institutions owned by wealthy people, who wish to lend primarily to the groups supporting them to consolidate their power and accumulate wealth. Hence, owners of banks are reluctant to extend credit to the poor. The behavior of the wealthy people will result in keeping the low-income groups out of the credit market.

A few individuals within low-income groups, however, would be in a position to neutralize the bankers' intentions of not granting loans to them, by offering collateral to secure loans. Consequently, the vast majority of the poor who do not have enough collateral to offer are denied access to credit. On the other hand, low income earners may not borrow as they cannot afford to pay the cost involved in borrowing, which is affected by the high transaction cost. Flow of money to poor people is also impeded because of the low financial literacy rates and lack of influential power they command within financial markets. In rural credit markets, finding guarantors acceptable to commercial banks is also a serious problem. In such circumstances, the poor remain poor over the period and therefore, the delivery of credit to the poor at subsidized rates would be required in order to create wealth for them. From a macroeconomic perspective, the income increase and wealth accumulation by the poor would result in a fair distribution of income.

c Structural weaknesses

Financial institutions managed by private parties aspire to earn profits and therefore, such institutions abstain from allocating resources to achieve social benefits. With the availability of limited resources, these institutions are reluctant to carry on with the burden of undertaking costly actions such as the evaluation and monitoring of small-scale projects. Uncertainty towards the stability and prospects of the economies of developing countries also influences banks to finance short term lucrative projects instead of micro level projects of the poor.

Financial literacy among the poor in developing countries remains rather low, which is a major drawback that adversely affects their capacity to make efficient and effective financial decisions. Further, lack of communication facilities, bank branches and complementary markets such as insurance markets, particularly in remote villages of developing countries badly affect the poor to access credit. The risk of providing loans associated with natural shocks such as bad weather conditions, also prevents lenders in curtailing credit. The poor in developing countries are adversely affected by such natural shocks, and lenders on the other hand do not have opportunities to diversify such risks because of the lack of development of credit markets.

Subsidized Interest Rates Versus Market Interest Rates

Low-income people, who are usually denied access to formal financial sources, would resort to MFIs for microfinance at low interest rates while expecting reasonably high rates of interest for their deposits. However, such a policy, if implemented, might weaken the leverage of the MFIs concerned, unless there is a flow of funds to the MFIs from donors, on a sustainable basis.

Under the above circumstances, the subsidized credits were extended to borrowers in many developing countries, through government sponsored programs that may include refinance schemes, interest rate subsidies and credit guarantee schemes. In spite of the fact that the intervention by the government in providing subsidized credit to low-income earners is justified through the economic efficiency argument and the income distribution argument, in practice, many credit programs implemented in developing countries have not produced expected results for various reasons.

The supply leading finance theory which proposes that finance should be provided in advance of the demand for the same, in order to achieve economic growth, provides a theoretical basis for the implementation of subsidized credit programs. However, this theory does not encapsulate the socio-economic context of rural poor and the conditions prevailing in the formal and informal rural financial markets. As described by Robinson (2001), the programs as a whole encountered widespread failures. Governments in many instances have maneuvered the credit programs to achieve certain political objectives, while the credit often did not reach the poor but ended up with large-scale borrowers and political supporters. A high default rate was a common feature of these subsidized credit schemes. No appropriate loan products were offered according to the needs of the borrowers, especially on time, and borrowers had to bear high transaction costs in securing the loans mainly due to cumbersome procedures involved in granting the loans.

Conversely, the non-poor have benefitted from the schemes mainly because the lending institutions have given emphasis towards lending to the rich clientele in the interest of addressing solvency issues. On the other hand, the lobbying by influential groups has also resulted in the programs not achieving intended targets. As a result, the distribution of income was often achieved regressively rather than progressively. Paying of low interest on savings of low income earners and the misuse of subsidized credit eventually created a complex situation which could not be explainable by the theory.

There is a school of thought that believes that small-scale borrowers are able to pay market interest rates while increasing their output and profits. Consequently, this could be further interpreted as that the grant of subsidized credit may act as a development constraint rather than a facilitator. However, Morduch and Armendariz (2011) consider that low income earners are unable to sustain themselves by taking loans at higher rates of interest, as their projects can generate only lower marginal return than the return of large-scale projects.

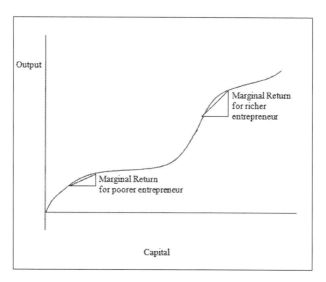

Figure 2.2 Marginal Returns for Poorer and Richer Entrepreneurs
Source: Morduch and Armendariz (2011)

According to Figure 2.2, if everything (such as education levels, business savvy, commercial contacts and access to inputs) is constant for both the richer and poorer borrowers except capital, then the marginal return (MR) for entrepreneurs with less capital could be lower than that of richer entrepreneurs.

A considerable number of people in the poverty group would plausibly be screened out on account of high interest rates, given the fact that these people generate low return on investment. However, the principle of diminishing marginal return may not be the case, even when the non-capital characteristics are alike for both the poor and the rich, because the production functions may not be 'conveniently' concave as illustrated by Armendariz and Morduch (2011, 18-19). Figure 2.2 shows that at a certain space, production technology exhibits increasing returns to scale, which in the context of investment, indicates that the large-scale entrepreneurs get larger profits relative to the returns of small-scale entrepreneurs.

In the past, certain borrowers who received subsidized loans could not generate enough income and therefore, their presence in the market did not contribute in any significant way to financial sector development. These negative outcomes experienced in practice could contribute to assert that the institutions which were operating under market principles, such as the grant of loans and mobilization of savings at market rates of interest, are better at having an impact on the income increases of the borrowers. This seems to be a plausible judgment mainly on the basis that only a small proportion of borrowers were said to have shifted to commercial banks in order to seek large-scale loans having improved their income under concessionary loan schemes.

Finally, subsidized credit did not appear to be a useful approach in rectifying the non-financial or financial distortions prevailing in rural credit markets. Conversely, the low interest credit has brought about many unintended side-effects and has not been effective in stimulating economic growth as expected, according to the supply leading finance theory. Further, rising costs, fungibility of credit and difficulty in the detection of the use of credit have made offsetting of the distortions infeasible. It was only useful as a second-best option, an inefficient way of addressing market failures. The implementation of subsidized credit programs would have suppressed the possible emergence of sustainable microfinance institutions in developing countries. However, MFIs have designed their operations gradually, adopting different types of lending models and thus facing the challenges successfully.

Strategic Options

As there are credit market failures, MFIs face an uphill task of gathering correct information on their customers and their projects. In this backdrop, an MFI should be able to decide on its strategic direction and continue to pursue it in achieving its goals. The strategic status of an MFI can be gauged by identifying the MFI's point of existence on a hypothetical line drawn between financial systems approaches to poverty lending approach.

The financial performance of a banking institution can be defined as the extent to which the full cost of providing services is directly paid for by service recipients (Yaron 1992). In contrast, the most common indicators used to define social performance are, the number of people using the financial services within a given period (breadth of outreach), the level of involvement by financial institutions in changing the poverty status of the poor (depth of outreach) and the net benefits that society accumulates (quality of outreach) through financial interventions.

There are various ways by which an MFI can shift its direction between financial performance and social performance. For instance, raising interest rates assuming that inelastic demand prevails, could improve financial performance, sometimes at the expense of social performance. Therefore, many decisions of MFIs would entail a trade-off between the social performance and financial performance over time.

Copestake (2007) has shown the strategic options available to an MFI in a diagrammatic form as indicated below.

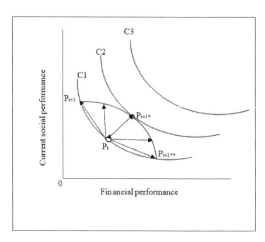

Figure 2.3 Strategic Options for MFIs
Source: Copestake (2007)

C1, C2 and C3 are indifference curves[8], each representing a set of combinations of social and financial performance, equally attractive to an MFI. The initial level of performance of an MFI is at P_t and the next time the MFI is constrained in how it can change its position within the performance possibility locus through policy changes, operational changes, innovations, investments and growth. The horizontal and vertical axes represent *growth-first* and *clients-first* strategies respectively. The line $P_{t\ to}\ P_{t+1*}$ is an intermediate strategy. The line moving up and to the left (towards P_{t+1}) shows a *trade-off* strategy that has improved social performance (e.g., increased rate of subsidies), while the downward sloping arrow (towards P_{t+1**}) represents a reduction in current social performance in order to achieve financial performance (e.g., targeting richer deliberately).

One of the most important ideas presented in Figure 2.3 is that, an MFI has the choice to decide whether it needs to move upward or downward along the indifference curve, from the point where it conducts an intermediate strategy.

ASYMMETRIC INFORMATION PARADIGM

In explaining the role of asymmetric information in credit markets on the lending practices of banks, Stiglitz and Weiss (1981) provide some pioneering views. In credit markets, asymmetric information refers to a situation where one party, is having more information than the other party when both are involved in a transaction. For instance, banks know little about investment choices, honesty, risk tolerance capacity and willingness to repay loans by the loan applicant (Robinson 2001, 128-129), attributes of which also vary depending on the character of the individual concerned. The capacity

---

[8] In any combination of choices represented at each point of an indifference curve, the user gets the same utility. In this particular case, the MFI (user) is indifferent in choosing any combination of financial gains and social gains along the indifference curve.

of financial institutions to observe these issues and understand them is restricted due to the cost factor. This incapacity of the banks to get full information of their clients often results in sub optimal allocation of financial resources.

Certain financial institutions, have also switched to sustain from the income generated from credit extended to the clientele with whom they place some trust. Sriram (2005) indicates that trust is a function of increased information and thus plays a significant role in determining transaction costs related to documentation and the delay in granting the loan. Therefore, the availability of information on potential customers is crucial in the determination of the type of contracts to be entered into with different types of clients, including the prices (interest rates) to be attached to the contract. In this context, success in the business of banking, to a larger extent, lies on the success of managing information about the customer. In other words, financial institutions should be able to make a good assessment on the level of risk of their potential customers.

Information flow in credit markets, especially in rural credit markets is imperfect. Individual borrowers are better informed about the projects they wish to undertake than the banks which would finance the projects. In particular, the banks may be ill informed about the position of the borrowers especially about their equity portions, investment choices, repayment capacities, honesty, risk tolerance etc. On the other hand, some banks are better informed than their competitors about prospective customers and their projects. These situations are examples of asymmetric information prevailing in the credit market. The salient feature of information asymmetry is that one party possesses more information than the other party about the transactions they do with each other.

The banks in developing countries are also separated from prospective clients by many other factors such as geographical distance and financial illiteracy that exists among poor communities. Credit information systems are unavailable or ineffective in bridging the information gap remaining between the poor and the lending institutions.

The problems of information asymmetry may not affect the informal or village money lenders seriously, as they have easier and accurate access to information on borrowers. Effective information accessibility enables the informal money lender to record lower default rates compared with the default rates of formal financial institutions (Braverman and Guasch 1986).

The microfinance industry suffers various market failures such as poverty reduction actions, availability of subsidies including informational disadvantages according to Porteous (2006). In information asymmetry, emphasis is given to three main areas, namely adverse selection, moral hazard and strategic default. Credit markets in developing countries suffer heavily due to these problems and therefore MFIs operating in developing countries need to understand such realities in advance. In view of this, research on microfinance has paid attention to microfinance models involving credit contracts, such as '*joint liability*' and '*dynamic incentives*' and their implications, in addressing the problems of adverse selection and moral hazard.

Adverse Selection

Adverse selection arises before contractual arrangements take place. Stiglitz and Weiss (1981) present a number of adverse selection models, setting off a new wave of ideas on this subject. With regard to credit markets, adverse selection mainly refers to the possession of insufficient information by banks, on the potential risks of the borrowers' creditworthiness and the projects to be undertaken by them. Most financial institutions in developing countries face the difficulty of observing the differences in credit quality of each borrower due to the absence of credit histories and collateral possessed by each of them.

The adverse selection models are discussed under *agency theory* in the literature. Coperstake (2007) describes the situation of adverse selection in terms of this theory in which directors set performance goals and managers as agents make decisions, and the outcome of the decisions is monitored systematically. Under a perfect information scenario, managers perform a role exactly as wanted by directors. However, the gap between 'perfect' position and actual position would be very wide in microfinance as the owners of MFIs are seriously handicapped by the lack of accurate and timely information. As indicated by Coperstake (2007, 1725), "*at worst owners' goals and preferences change opportunistically in response to actual performance outcomes (agents) rather than being a fixed point against which performance can be guided and assessed.*"

In practice, lending institutions adopt different strategies to protect themselves from problems of information asymmetry; they would charge equally high rates of interest from all the borrowers equally without making an attempt to differentiate the high-risk individuals from the low-risk individuals (Armendariz and Morduch 2011; Robinson 2001). Consequently, the high-risk individuals will be willing to obtain the loans while the low-risk individuals choose not to borrow. Subsequently, the average riskiness in respect of the loan applicant pool goes up and banks will be placed at a disadvantaged position. On the other hand, borrowers who take loans at high rates of interest have no option but to choose risky projects expecting high returns although, there is also a high probability of default corresponding to investments in risky projects.

The decrease in expected returns with the increase in average riskiness of loans under the high interest rate option, might compel lending institutions to change their strategy and apply low rates of interest on loans. As the price of money goes down, the demand for credit increases. Banks would implement a policy by which credit rationing is introduced, and as a consequence, some of the low income people would be denied credit. On the other hand, banks, without changing the rate of interest, could demand collateral from the borrowers in order to offset the riskiness of loans. The flow of credit to the poor is badly affected by this strategy, although, it might improve the credit recovery. The average riskiness of the borrowings of banks would go down sharply when collateral is obtained for the loans granted.

Godwin (2004) shows how credit rationing is possible if an MFI is aware of the borrower type, which is illustrated in Figure 2.4.

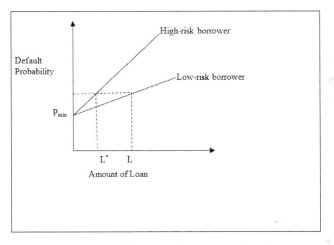

Figure 2.4 Default Probability, Credit Risk and the Loan Amount
Source: Godquin (2004)

The repayment probability decreases in proportion to the level of risk of the borrower. The minimal probability of default, P_{min} is a result of the borrower facing unforeseen external factors such as the destruction of the project assets or incapacitation of borrower due to illness etc. With the observation that the repayment probability varies on the basis of the level of risk, the MFI will ration the credit, i.e., L amount of credit to safer borrowers and L* amount of credit to risky borrowers.

MFIs have devised certain innovative means, such as joint liability GLSs, to address the problems of information asymmetries and its implication on the trade-off between financial sustainability and the outreach of microfinance programs (Hermes and Lensink 2007). GLSs are considered effective in mitigating the adverse selection problem by their widespread use by many MFIs in developing countries. Ghatak (1999) also argues that group lending can solve the problem of lenders as the risky and safe borrowers group into one, which is homogenous to each other. However, Guttman (2008) suggests that positive assortative matching does not necessarily hold true if the lending is extended incorporating dynamic incentives. As the group lending scheme is supposed to provide a close relationship with the theme of this research the Guttman (2007) analysis on the behavior of risky and safe borrowers is illustrated below.

It is assumed that there are two types of borrowers; risky borrowers (type x) and safe borrowers (type y).

Probability of success of the borrower pi (i=x, y) where $p_x < p_y$.

There are two Assumptions: a). success or failure of each borrower's project is uncorrelated with the others and

b), when project succeeds, income = D >0 and if it fails income = 0

The loan taken by each borrower is to be repaid with the principal plus interest so that one unit of repayment is k>1. Assuming that two members form a group and undertake to pay c (degree of joint liability) if one of the co-members defaults and k and c are exogenous variables, and that both borrowers are risk-neutral, we could find the borrower i's expected payoff of taking a loan together with borrower j as follows:

$$E\pi_{ij} = p_i p_j (D-k) + p_i(1-p_j) \ (D-k-c)$$
$$= p_i(D-k) - p_i(1-p_j) \ c \tag{1}$$

The simplified equation (1) has two terms, the first being the borrower i's expected net payoff from his own project and the second term is the cost he is supposed to bear from the project of borrower j. This shows that the probability of the borrower i is required to pay as cost c is equal to the probability of his own project success (p_i) and the borrower j's project failure, i.e., $(1-p_j) = p_i (1-p_j)$ c.

The expected payoff to a safe borrower, of taking a loan together with another safe borrower is,

$$E\pi_{bb} = p_y p_y (D-k) + p_y (1-p_y)(D-k-c)$$
$$= p_y^2 c + p_y (D-k-c). \tag{2}$$

We can also find safe borrower's expected payoff of taking a loan with risky borrower as follows:

$$E\pi_{ba} = p_y p_x (D-k) + p_y (1-p_x)(D-k-c)$$
$$= p_y p_x c + p_y (D-k-c). \tag{3}$$

Subtracting (3) from (2), we get

$$E\pi_{yy} - E\pi_{yx} = p_y (p_y - p_x)c > 0 \tag{4}$$

The expression in equation (4) is the safe borrower's relative preference to form a group with another safe borrower. Similarly, the risky borrower's relative preference to form a group with a safe borrower is:

$$E\pi_{xy} - E\pi_{xx} = p_x (p_y - p_x)c > 0 \tag{5}$$

Both equations (4) and (5) are positive but (4) is larger than (5) as $p_y > p_x$.

The r.h.s. of (5) refers to the risky borrower's offer of payment to a safe borrower for accepting him as a co-member of the group. However, the safe borrower is willing to pay more, i.e., the r.h.s. of (4) for having another safe borrower as his partner rather than a risky borrower. This shows that in group formation, risky borrowers are forced to form groups with similar borrower types whereas safe borrowers are also willing to group with similar type of safe borrowers.

Even though the group lending programs in developing countries, possibly allow risky and safe borrowers to sort themselves into relatively homogenous groups and this positive assortative matching is exploited by lenders to avoid adverse selection problems, this expectation does not hold true under certain conditions (Guttman 2008). Laffont and N'Guessan (2000) also present a theoretical model to show that if the borrowers are not known to each other, the adverse selection cannot be a foundation of group lending. In this context, group lending is not considered to be a panacea for all problems emanating from information asymmetries.

There is also a possibility that the adverse selection problem would increase along with the increase in competition among MFIs. McIntosh and Wydick (2005) suggest that competition among MFIs complicate the ability to gauge the indebtedness of the borrower and as a result risky borrowers tend to obtain multiple loans thus creating less beneficial loan contracts for all borrowers. This happens because MFIs being unable to find two types of borrowers distinctively, apply high rates of interest on each and every loan in order to safeguard themselves against the possible risk. Overall, the rural credit markets in developing countries operate under a lack of information systems, while the competition leaves the good customers at a vulnerable position due to the actions of risky customers. According to Luoto, Mcintosh and Wydick (2007), competition among MFIs has led to increased indebtedness, decrease in loan repayment incentives and the buildup of arrears as there is an absence of information sharing in these markets. This research further points out that the credit information systems can play a role in improving credit market performance and estimates that screening effects from the credit market system helped decrease arrears.

Moral Hazard

The problem of moral hazard is defined in terms of two types - *Ex ante* moral hazard and *Ex post* moral hazard by Armendariz and Morduch (2011). Accordingly, *Ex ante* moral hazard refers to a situation where lenders cannot observe actions taken by the borrower after the loan has been taken but before the returns on projects are realized. The lack of information prevents the lender from finding out how the borrower has devoted to promote the project for which the money has been obtained. On the other hand, *Ex post* moral hazard refers to banks' difficulty in observing borrower's actions after the loan is granted and project returns are realized. In the '*agency theory*' on credit markets, this situation is often referred to as a '*take the money and run*' problem.

Applying the moral hazard problem to microfinance, Robinson (2001, 155) describes that

> The limited liability of borrowers (agents) – especially when found in conjunction with the higher interest rates charged by banks (principals) – may result in high-risk investments by borrowers whose liability is limited and who may expect to default on their loans if their investments fail (moral hazard).

In the absence of collateral, lending institutions' charging of high rates of interest on all loans would be counterproductive, as the high-risk individuals who receive loans would pay little attention to the productive use of the loan. There is no mechanism or capacity to monitor individual investments, particularly for micro loans. Consequently, the borrowers often choose to invest in high-risk projects while taking action to hide performance details about the project from the lender.

This moral hazard action of the borrower is induced when the exchange of transaction is not supported by adequate collateral. The peer monitoring system introduced in joint liability schemes and awareness programs, conducted by MFIs to inculcate good ethics of banking, would be useful in addressing the moral hazard problem to some extent. Simtowe, Zeller and Phiri (2006) examine the extent of the occurrence of moral hazard and its determinants of occurrence within a joint liability lending program in Malawi and show that peer selection, peer monitoring and peer pressure, dynamic incentives and other factors that capture the extent of matching problems account for a greater part of variation in the incidence of moral hazard among credit groups. The policy implication of the research is that lending institutions which practice joint liability, need to depend on social cohesion to reduce the incidence of moral hazard and thereby, achieve the objectives of outreach, impact and sustainability satisfactorily.

There is some complexity over the clear demarcation of hidden information (adverse selection) and hidden action (moral hazard). Using a field experiment methodology to estimate the presence and importance of hidden information and hidden action problems in a consumer credit market, Karlan and Zinman (2009) have attempted to disentangle the hidden information from the hidden action effect, based on a theoretical model formalized for this purpose. The experiment conducted on a sample of successful prior borrowers by a for-profit lender in a high-risk South African consumer market suggests that there is weak evidence of hidden information but strong evidence of moral hazard, accounting for 13 percent to 21 percent of defaults of clients.

Strategic Default

The term strategic default refers to a situation where borrowers provide false information to banks about the profitability of their projects in order to not repay the loans. Both the adverse selection problem and the moral hazard problem increase the chances of defaults by the borrower. If the lending banks increase the interest rates to cover the risk, owing to asymmetric information on the borrower, the high-risk borrowers would take the loans and invest them on high-risk projects. As a result, the likelihood that the borrower will default the loan would be very high. With regard to microfinance, the poor borrowers have only a limited liability as they often lack collateral to offer in getting a loan. Knowing this position of the borrowers, the MFIs that adopt a poverty lending approach usually grant loans to them without demanding collaterals in the form of assets. In such circumstances, the borrowers are not affected due to their hiding of information on the return of the investments with a view of not repaying loans.

There are limitations under GLSs to tackle the problem of strategic default successfully. However, group lending operations could be designed dynamically in order to suit the local conditions under which the groups are required to operate. Bhole and Ogden (2010) show that the problem of strategic default cannot be addressed successfully even under GLSs, unless group members can impose social sanctions that are costly on one another, or unless the financial institution uses a cross reporting methodology. They suggest a flexible group lending contract, in which the amount that a successful borrower is obliged to pay for a defaulting co-member when optimally determined, while the penalty is left to vary across group members, has some advantages. Through an investigation of impact on the repayment rate of loans granted to groups that are made jointly liable, Besley and Coate (1995) have observed the presence of positive and negative impact but, group lending harnessing social collateral could serve to reduce the negative impact. Armendariz (1999) provides details on the optimal design of collective agreements with joint liability in order to curtail the incidence of strategic defaults, implying that there are mixed results on repayment rates under GLSs.

SHOULD INFORMAL SECTOR LENDING BE CONTINUED?

Informal money lenders in developing countries play a significant role in the provision of credit to the poor. The formal sector, especially commercial banks, is reluctant to replace the money lenders' role mainly because that these banks lack the need or capability of determining the creditworthiness of the prospective borrowers of money lenders. Banks are keen on the availability of collateral and income generating capacity of the projects in order to ensure that there are no hassles in recovering the loans. They also consider the reliability of the enforcement capacities present in recovering loans from a defaulter. Money lenders approach these aspects in a more dynamic manner that is agreeable to the level of expectation of intended borrowers. MFIs on the other hand, may prefer to adopt hybrid approaches of lending, based both on the experience of banks and money lenders. MFIs therefore, are able to provide banking facilities to the people who are also in the same cluster of customers that would be served by the money lenders.

Informal sector money lending as a business has continued for decades in developing countries, although its impact on socio-economic aspects of borrowers and the formal banking system is not conclusive. As mentioned by Robinson (2001, 178-183), the importance of money lending in the rural credit market may be viewed under three different possibilities – as a malicious monopolistic action, as a good value for borrowers and as a type of monopolistic competition. Borrowers are in general subjected to very high interest rates as against lower transaction costs under informal money lenders, whereas under the formal banking system, borrowers face a contrasting situation; i.e., low interest rates as against high transaction costs. The point of interest here is the lower total cost to be borne by the borrower on a loan from a formal banking institution, as against the total cost of a loan from a money lender. It should be, however, noted that the low income groups are not in a position to reject high cost informal lending in order to replace it with low cost formal sector lending, for various reasons.

Money Lenders as Credit Facilitators

Although the money lenders presence in the market has irked policy makers, there is a school of thought which believes that the services offered by money lenders to low income rural households in developing countries are essential. Among the benefits available to the poor are the possibilities of entering into easy contracts, obtaining timely credit, selecting flexible repayment structures and providing less or no collateral in getting loans.

The representation by the money lenders in the market, particularly in terms of the value and volume of transactions involved as against the formal sector, is difficult to estimate, as the transactions often take place on a personal basis between the money lender and the borrower. Available data have shown development of formal financial sector institutions with a dramatic increase of the proportion of credit granted by them from 1950s to date, world over. However, it is a stylized fact that economies with less developed credit markets tend to occupy more segmented credit markets with a significant share from the informal market.

Under a monopolistic competitive environment, the price charged by the money lender is fixed above the market rates. This requires that an interest rate cap be put through the presence of the formal sector in credit markets. At the same time, MFIs presence in the market is also essential to protect the poor from money lenders' actions, specifically helping them escape from the alleged clutches of 'evil money lenders' as described by Meyer (2002).

The differences in the cost of screening, monitoring and contract enforcement also provide a theoretical basis for the co-existence of the informal and formal sector in rural credit markets (Hoff and Stiglitz 1998). Formal credit, granted at subsidized rates, generates a demand that requires financial institutions to ration the credit, and as a result, the formal sector credit becomes a function of the demand for credit and its availability from informal sources (Kochar, 1997). The point of interest here is that unlike commercial banks that ration credit resulting from information failure and lack of funds, money lenders are capable of meeting the credit requirements of the poor in its entirety. The presence of a dual market is unavoidable as formal sector loans favor only the wealthy borrowers while the majority of informal sector lenders cater to the needs of micro-level borrowers.

Money lenders in general include wealthy entrepreneurs, wholesale and retail traders, and other influential people in local rural markets. This group of people usually maintain a friendly relationship with the persons to whom they provide credit. For instance, these lenders may request collateral in the form of a future harvest, a note indicating an ownership transfer of some kind of asset in the event of default or similar things, which are agreeable to the borrowers. Although, this asymmetric interdependence may cause some problems to the borrowers at the end, as the weaker party, they have no other choice but to seek out assistance from the money lenders. Village money lenders have become one of the principal sources of credit to low-income groups whose projects in general are regarded as problematic due to low productivity, insufficient collateral and the high-risk of failure (including natural causes).

Money lenders usually have the advantage of using their position, influence, power and personal relationships, to obtain information on prospective borrowers, apply lower enforcement costs and differentiate their clients according to risk of default to sustain in rural credit markets. Hence, the informal sector players provide services to the poor in rural villages in a manner that could not be supplanted by the players from the formal sector. This situation leaves the credit markets in developing countries dichotomized into the 'formal' and 'informal' sectors.

Unreasonable Interest Rates

It is often considered that the money lenders charge high rates of interest from the borrowers, taking into account factors such as administrative costs, risk premium, probability of defaults, scarcity of capital, insufficient collateral and the opportunity cost of capital. High interest rates also result from exogenous factors such as the probable demand of loans for consumption purposes, seasonal character of demand, fewer facilities on geographic mobility, low income and education among borrowers etc. (Robinson 2001, 177). In view of this situation, money lenders are able to realize monopoly (or oligopoly) profits.

One of the strong arguments for the presence of formal sector financial institutions, including MFIs, is that they could play a key role in lowering the rate of interest prevailing in rural credit markets. Consequently, it is expected that poor people are protected from the so-called usurious interest rates charged by money lenders to some extent. There is evidence, however, to show that certain desired results expected through the availability of cheap credit to the poor have not been achieved. For instance, Hoff and Stiglitz (1998), by presenting some theoretical models, demonstrate that although informal money lenders who benefitted from subsidized interest rates, were expected to trickle down the benefits to the clients they serve, this would not happen. They contend that, due to endogenous enforcement costs, this effect is likely to be attenuated and may even be reversed. The underlying view behind this is that when the credit market is monopolistically competitive, free entry into money lending businesses takes place and the increase in the marginal cost of money due to some specific reasons (such as reduction of the market share, increase in enforcement efforts and cost of each money lender, and the rising cost of taking an additional customer by each money lender), will result in the equilibrium rate of interest going up.

If the demand for credit by some borrowers can be met in full by formal sector lending, there is a likelihood that the interest rates in the market would reduce under a perfect competitive situation. However, this downward pressure is not witnessed in a monopolistically competitive market where there is a possibility for free entry and imperfect substitutability of one money lender for another. Further, Mallick (2012), through an empirical research, suggests that an increase in microfinance coverage causes increases in money lenders' interest rates. This is because, when loans from MFIs are invested in productive purposes, the default risk lowers and interest rates charged by MFIs will also come down. However, as there is a limitation for formal sector credits, borrowers may resort to money lenders for additional requirements of money (investment, working capital, repaying the loan) and such demand for money may induce the money lenders to raise their interest rates.

Another aspect of rural credit market is the creditworthy borrowers' intention to shift to the formal sector, leaving only the risky borrowers for the money lenders. Money lenders add an appropriate risk premium, resulting in an increase in interest rates (Bose 1998; Hoff and Stiglitz 1998). The informal sector also suffers from the problems associated with the handling of small-scale loans. In this connection, there is a belief that scale advantages of the formal sector outweigh the informational advantages of local money lenders. Further, the expansion of formal lending may create less benefit for the borrowers from the informal sector, as the strengthening of the formal sector would lead to a collusion among the informal lenders (Floro and Ray 1997).

As Robinson (2001) highlights, the charging of high interest rates could be viewed from three areas of reasoning, which have some theoretical foundation. Firstly, under the 'malicious' monopolistic money lender who charges high interest rates while earning exorbitant profits, borrowers do not have the opportunity to negotiate with terms and conditions of the loan. This situation might lead borrowers to repay the loans in the form of assets or bonded labor. The charging of monopsony prices and land alienation are common problems with these money lenders. There are money lenders who would create value for people through the carrying out of a legitimate business at reasonable interest earnings. In such instances, the cost of transaction and high-risk that are to be borne by the lender are not exploitive or malicious. Under monopolistic competition, there are large numbers of money lenders present in rural credit markets, providing services that are similar but not in perfect substitutability. If a lender raises the interest rate relative to the interest rates of competitors, the grant of credit is not affected significantly. Under monopolistic competition, there is also a possibility of easy entry, product specialization and geographical separation of the service. Lenders can earn economic profit in the short run, but because of the free entry into the market, individual lenders' profits are driven down and as a result there is no way of earning economic profits over the long run.

Lessons for MFIs

An MFI may obtain funds for its operation through various sources such as borrowings, equity capital, grants and savings mobilized from clients. On the other hand, the informal sector lenders use their own money and funds collected from many other known and friendly sources, except the deposits from clients, which they may not be able to mobilize due to legal constraints. Therefore, the cost of capital for both the money lenders and MFIs should be viewed with the understanding of their respective sources of funds.

Some MFIs may be able to mobilize funds from clients and extend credits to prospective borrowers under the terms and conditions that match the terms and conditions of credit of money lenders. Further, MFIs can choose to adopt the same strategies that money lenders adopt, in accessing potential clients and granting loans to them accordingly. For instance, MFIs can design low cost products according to the needs of the clients and offer the same at minimal transaction costs. They also can build up personal relationships with customers, as done by money lenders. Other procedures such as the timely delivery of credit and flexible methods for the recovery of loans may also be adopted by MFIs. These competitive strategies are useful in convincing the customers that they would be better served through the MFIs.

MFIs are not in a position to supplant the role of informal money lenders, whose services towards the poor comprise many unique features that are advantageous to borrowers. However, from government policy perspectives, it is necessary to implement strategies that would facilitate formal financial institutions to operate successfully. If money lenders are malicious with the intention of granting loans, expecting excessive benefits such as bonded labor and land alienation, an appropriate policy level intervention is necessary to rectify the situation. It is useful to encourage MFIs to intervene in the market in such occasions. On the other hand, if money lenders perform their operations creating value for the people, MFIs need to take appropriate actions that would not be detrimental to the activities of such money lenders. Finally, however, with the presence of monopolistic competition, banks and MFIs would need to be encouraged to grant money at lower rates of interest for the benefit of the poor.

MICRO SAVINGS AND THE POOR

Savings of comparatively small amounts are referred to as micro savings. In rural credit markets, the financial institutions pay considerable attention to the savings component of low income earners, before granting any loans to them. This is because savings are considered to be an initial first step towards the start of a viable project by a small entrepreneur. The average amount of savings of the poor, is usually small, mainly due to their low earnings and irregular income flows. Savings, are therefore, important in cushioning against the exigencies of low income people. Panda (2010, 11-12), outlines several advantages of micro savings. For instance, as the income flow of the poor is irregular and seasonal, meeting their expenditure on a daily and weekly basis would be easier under some mechanism of saving. Besides, savings are also helpful to the poor in order to protect themselves from the usurious interest rates charged by money lenders, who usually attach difficult conditions along with credit. When/if the future income decreases for some reason, the savings at present would be useful to avoid any fluctuation in the consumption patterns of individuals at any future date. Further, the savings would promote the self-esteem of the poor, giving them some status and voice in their own community and society in general.

Determinants of Savings

The prime determinant of savings is income. The other variables such as interest rates, inflation and tax rates may also be influential in determining the amount of savings. Although, savings are dependent on income, the amount of savings of each individual could be determined by his or her future income expectation and requirements to protect against anticipated future expenditure. Also, the need for liquidity to meet the exigencies of life, due to the perceived risk of losing labor income, is an important factor that influences savings. In low income countries, a critical factor that influences savings is lifetime expenditures like housing, consumer durables and sometimes the setting up of small businesses (Athukorala and Sen 2002).

The Forgotten Half of Microfinance

Savings are one of the prerequisites for obtaining loans from many MFIs. As microfinance has evolved, the importance of savings has been recognized increasingly, which is often referred to as the forgotten half of microfinance. Generating income through the projects financed by MFIs and managing household income and expenditure in a prudent manner are important steps towards building up household savings.

Savings can be promoted on a voluntary basis or as 'forced savings' in which borrowers are required to put aside a fixed percentage of their borrowing as savings. In any case, savings have been an important factor in the microfinance sector for a few reasons. Savings provide funds for MFIs at a cheaper rate of interest compared with the interest rates of commercial borrowings. Hence, MFIs can use savings mobilized from the poor for the purpose of lending at low interest rates. Savings can be an instrument that would be useful in reaching the poor and achieving the sustainability of MFIs. Through savings, MFIs create a pool of depositors who would become borrowers at a future date and these depositors may be able to use their savings as collateral in obtaining loans. The savings mobilization may also help in information processing in respect of granting loans, and transferring benefits to MFIs in the form of cost mitigation.

Policymakers and bankers in many developing countries are of the impression that the poor do not save, cannot save, do not trust financial institutions and prefer nonfinancial forms of savings (Robinson 1994b). In this context, MFIs have observed the importance of savings by the poor and designed appropriate strategies that could influence the poor to save. If the poor have sufficient incomes, the most influential factor of savings could be the offering of attractive interest rates for their deposits. However, regulations governing the involvement of MFIs in savings programs are also critical in the mobilization of deposits.

MFIs are eager to differentiate the cost between the funds collected from donors and savings mobilized from the poor. However, it has been accepted that in the interest of sustainability, MFIs need to depend on savings mobilization. In this connection, the MFIs should not consider opportunity cost of funds as an important factor considering the social cost of subsidization.

IS CREDIT TO THE POOR CHALLENGING?

Financial services extended by formal financial institutions, among others include the analysis of risk profiles of the projects concerned and understanding of authentic information on transaction history and expected behavior of the customer. These tasks pose challenges to MFIs which have become a major force in extending finance to the poor, in an environment where there are market failures. Gonzalez-Vega (1998) identifies systemic risks, increasing competition, improper regulation and the return of the state as the areas that pose considerable threats to the development of microfinance. In these circumstances, MFIs also have become more dynamic in calculating and mitigating the risks of their clients.

Viewpoints of Welfarists and Institutionalists

The programs implemented by MFIs were more or less subsidized in the 1990s, underpinning their importance as a means of addressing poverty. However, by today, the microfinance industry experiences a new wave of challenges. The central issue among them could be the achievement of sustainability by MFIs as against the poverty reduction of their clients. In this connection, the use of the market rate of interest versus subsidized rates on loans, and the application of regulations, prudential or otherwise versus the non-application of the same have become some of the issues intensely debated at present.

Beginning in the 1990s, a large and diverse body of empirical literature has investigated trade-off between poverty outreach and the sustainability of MFIs (Quayes 2012; Hermes, Lensink, and Meesters 2011; Mersland and Strom 2010; Weiss and Montgomery 2005; Schreiner 2002; Robinson 2001; Morduch 2000). There has been no consensus among analysts on the expected relationship between outreach and sustainability. In policy circles, the issue has been transformed into an intense debate between welfarists who argue for achieving the outreach objective (Woller 2002; Weiss and Montegomery 2005) and institutionalists who stress the importance of achieving sustainability and efficiency (Rhyne 1998, Christen 2000). Welfarists focus on the depth of poverty outreach, and believe that financial services should be extended to improve the level of income of poor, aiming at alleviating poverty. In addressing the depth of poverty, welfarists also place emphasis on women empowerment, education of children of the poor etc., which, however, could be possible through MFIs, only if they receive some form of financial grants and subsidized funds. Institutionalists, on the other hand, focus on the breadth of outreach, requiring MFIs to expand financial services to a large number of people. These MFIs are concerned with the repaying capacity of their clients more than addressing their level of poverty. This approach could help MFIs to sustain profits, thereby strengthening the financial deepening of the markets.

The arguments of welfarists versus institutionalists are described under two broader concepts; the poverty lending approach and the financial systems approach as outlined by Robinson (2001). The MFIs that adopt the former have to depend mainly upon donor-funds to extend credit to the poor, particularly to the poorest segment of the population as against the MFIs that follow the latter approach. The point that needs attention here is that both approaches are similar as far as their primary focus is concerned, i.e., ensuring the availability of financial services to a wider section of the poor in order to improve their standards of living.

A significant level of sustainability in microfinance could only be achieved through the adoption of a financial systems approach, according to Robinson (2001). In contrast, a question is also raised whether MFIs could strike a balance between the two approaches, i.e., achieving sustainability and reaching poverty groups simultaneously through a sound banking policy. Do poverty outreach and sustainability function complementarily, particularly in the context of achieving economies of scale and cost reduction by MFIs through the servicing of a larger numbers of clients? Woller, Dunford and Woodworth (1999) stress that the views of the two opposing camps are not inherently incompatible although there can be a substantial rift between the two camps. In fact, many MFIs in practice seem to embrace both approaches.

Empirical Insights

Some of the empirical findings of the microfinance studies provide very useful guidance in pursuit of the objectives of this research. Quayes (2012) for instance, having conducted a research utilizing a large and extensive sample of 702 MFIs operating in 83 countries, affirms that there is a complementary positive relationship between the depth of outreach and financial sustainability of MFIs, if they fulfil certain preconditions such as the application of sound banking practices. In contrast, Hermes, Lensink and Meesters (2011) contend that outreach is negatively related to the efficiency of MFIs (analyzing operations of 435 MFIs spanning over a period of 11 years) and the granting of small loans and serving of more women borrowers (measures of the depth of outreach) are less efficient in terms of achieving sustainability. According to them, the increase in efficiency can only be achieved if MFIs focus less on the poor.[9] Morduch (2000, 618-619), suggests that a *'win-win'* proposition with regard to the targeting of poverty and improving institutional capacity with the use of "best practices, such as financial transparency, standardizing products, and achieving scale" is neither supported by logic nor any empirical evidence. The study maintains that profit maximization is not the only way to make a program successful and the MFIs need to give emphasis towards the development of new products that are financially sustainable, while keeping a budget constraint in place when programs are implemented.

---

[9] This study heavily relies on the *Stochastic Frontier Analysis* to determine the cost efficiency of an MFI.

There is a widely held view in the literature that profit seeking MFIs have the tendency to find new markets and be more efficient (Christen and Drake 2002; Rhyne 1998). Maintaining the same line of thought, Mersland and Strøm (2010) indicate that as profits and costs may outweigh each other, there cannot be a mission drift. For instance, it has been found that an average loan size increases with an increase in average profits and average operational costs. The study predicts that efforts to reduce costs are very effective in reaching poorer segments and recommends that MFIs focus attention on achieving cost efficiency rather than concentrating on commercialisation.com

The poverty impact of the operations of MFIs could also be measured in terms of different criteria, in addition to the depth of outreach. For instance, Navajas et al. (2000, 344) stress that improved social conditions under microcredit depend not only on depth but also on several other factors such as its worth and cost to users, and its breadth, length, and scope of output, based on a theoretical framework and study of five MFIs in Bolivia. According to the research, the most important pursuit of MFIs, the depth of outreach, could be constrained by the increasing administrative cost, which is largely dependent on the amount of transaction costs.

The law of decreasing unit transaction costs on larger size transactions are also important in understanding possible trade-offs between outreach and the sustainability of MFIs. Empirical evidence shows that transaction costs of MFIs have a large fixed cost component. In obtaining information useful for the determination of the creditworthiness of poor clients, MFIs usually need to spend a substantial amount of cost. This will result in per unit cost of small loans to increase in a situation where a large portion of fixed cost has already been added irrespective of the size of the loan. This makes the granting of smaller loans less cost effective than the granting of larger loans. Many analysts (Schreiner 2002, Morduch 2000, Rhyne 1998) also identify that the high transaction cost per smaller sized loan is one of the main challenges faced by MFIs.

There is some general consensus that very poor borrowers have limited opportunities available for them to improve their income levels. Mosley and Hulme (1998), having studied 13 MFIs in seven developing countries that includes Sri Lanka, reaffirm that MFIs which focus their lending on the poorest segment make a relatively low impact on household income, but those which focus on the not-so-poor are more successful in improving the income of the clients. The low income has compelled poor clients to disregard investing in new technology and fixed investments, thereby diverting their interest towards working capital investments and consumption requirements. On the other hand, loans to higher income groups are considered to be effective in generating more income as, most often, such loans are utilized on viable projects.

MFIs that adopt more market friendly designs in operations have the advantage of assessing the creditworthiness of the clients with criteria available within the market system itself. For instance, the application of the market rate of interest would be useful in screening out borrowers whose rate of return on the project seem to be low and the financial discipline and quality of collateral they possess seem to be questionable. The poorest of the poor are eventually left out from the loan market due to such practices. In this backdrop, Mosley and Hulme (1998) state that task of MFIs in servicing the poor can be maximized through appropriate innovations with regard to the institutional design, certain modifications to savings and loans and incentives offered to borrowers as well as their own staff. Cull, Demirguc-Kunt and Morduch (2009, 190-191) also point out that there is a need for MFIs to be sustainable institutions that apply market principles while developing innovations such as new loan products and savings products, in order to reach poor effectively. According to their research, subsidization is not a practical alternative to profit maximization.

The lending policies of MFIs should facilitate the process for the poor to obtain finances without much hassle and start projects that could improve their income level, at least in the long-run. Montegomery and Weiss (2011), having studied nearly 3000 borrowers of the largest MFI that operated in Pakistan under commercial principles (Khushhali Bank), contend that the lending approach of the MFI has been helpful for poverty reduction, empowerment of women and the improvement of the health of children. As highlighted by this research, the general argument, that commercially oriented microfinance cannot reach the poorest because those people lack financial discipline (Hulme and Mosley 1998) and that they are risk averse to integrate with the programs in the same way as other borrowers, is debatable.

Many studies have given emphasis on the introduction of innovations to products and internal operations of MFIs in order to mitigate the trade-off between efficiency and poverty outreach (Hulme 2000; Morduch 2000; Hulme and Mosley 1998). Hermes and Lensink (2007) state that MFIs that operate focusing on individuals may perform better in terms of profitability, while MFIs that focus on group-based operations could perform better in terms of serving women borrowers and the poor. Armendariz and Morduch (2011) indicate that giving emphasis towards the use of group lending and other innovative approaches to reach the poor is an effective way of ensuring repayment.

The profit seeking strategy of MFIs would eventually help improving the socio-economic conditions of the poor, although there is no consensus on the matter among researchers who have dealt with the subject. For instance, views of Cull, Demirguc-Kunt and Morduch (2009) do not agree with Rosengard (2004) who describes that the profit motive and development impact of MFIs reinforce each other and eventually there is a synergy creation that would address both self-interest and community interest. It can be seen that there is ample room for different approaches to be adopted in the provision of microfinance services, relying on mainly the poverty focused models as well as financial efficiency focused models. It shows that the most important point is the application of institutional diversification, product differentiation, and market segmentation, in order to reach the poor effectively (Rosengard 2004, 33).

Innovations by MFIs to reduce costs could result in achieving both financial sustainability and social performance. These innovations should comprise all levels of operations of MFIs, from strategic planning to post implementation stages of planning. As suggested by Copestake (2007, 1723-1731), social performance can be improved through servicing more clients, broadening the availability of financial services, servicing a longer period and ensuring that the services offered do not harm the progress of the poor in any way. It is further suggested in the research that better targeting of the poor, flexible and diversified services available to the clients, staff selection and training given to them, quality of external relationships the MFIs maintained with other commercial and non-commercial organizations are all critical factors that ensure the eventual success of MFIs.

Certain MFIs have experimented with the adoption of commercial banking approaches, which include activities such as lending money by way of overdraft, and extending various other facilities to the poor such as guarantees, performance bonds, and safekeeping of documents. Further, they also provide advisory services on investment, conduct insurance and sales activities of various forms purely in order to improve their financial sustainability.

Subsidized Funds and Subsidized Credit

One of the key thoughts of efficiency versus outreach of MFIs is that MFIs should continue to depend upon subsidized funds rather than mobilized funds from the market at market rates of interest. According to Morduch (1999), as the credit markets in developing countries function imperfectly, the provision of interest subsidies to MFIs could be helpful in finding the allocative efficiency as the second best option. Hudon and Traca (2011) affirm that small subsidies given to MFIs, to a certain extent, could lead to increase their productivity than those MFIs which do not receive subsidies. The main argument in this case is that such subsidies allow MFIs to improve their physical and human resources capacity and efficiency even though there are limits to such improvements, resulting from subsidies.

It was the practice during the 1960s and the 1970s that credits to the poor were granted at low rates of interest, although the schemes benefited non-poor as well. These subsidized credits have also led to the very poor becoming continuous dependents who made no serious efforts to rise above poverty. This is why Morduch (2000) suggests that absolute cheap credit should be at a modest level, targeting only the poor.

HAS THERE BEEN A MISSION DRIFT?

Studies analyzing the 'mission drift' in microfinance describe the term in a nutshell as the leaving aside of the poorest by MFIs in order to achieve sustainability. The mission drift, as a concept, emanates out of the extended debate of financial efficiency versus poverty outreach. MFIs are a type of institutions whose mission is defined to include the large-scale poverty reduction of the poor and the servicing of unbanked people in rural areas. However, some of these MFIs, in order to achieve financial sustainability, have scaled up their operations. This shifting of operations with a focus on the achievement of profits has to be viewed in the light of the original mission of an MFI concerned, in order to ascertain whether there has been a mission drift.

The literature on mission drift in microfinance is reasonably rich (Mersland and Strøm 2010; Kumar Kar 2010; Hishigsuren 2007), but most of the empirical studies are country-specific so that they provide diverse views on the subject of mission drift. Empirical evidence supports that the MFIs that pay attention to serve up market clients could easily fall into the mission drift trap. One way of measuring the effectiveness of the mission of a poverty focused MFI is to identify how small is the average size of its loan. It is presumed that the smaller the average loan size, the greater the depth of outreach in terms of the operations of microfinance. Conversely, with the increase of the size of the average loan, it is generally accepted that the original mission is less underscored by MFIs.

In contrast to the general views highlighted above, Armendariz and Szafarz (2009) indicate that the increase in the average size of loan results from two main reasons, progressive lending (increasing the size of the loan based on the repayment of the loan by the client at the end of each credit cycle) and cross-subsidization (reaching unbanked wealthier customers). After studying MFIs operating in Latin America and South Asia, these researchers have indicated the difficulty in finding out whether the mission drift has actually taken place or not and suggested that monopolistic interest rates, together with average loan size, could be an indication of mission drift, provided the poorer clients have been crowded out by wealthier clients in this exercise. Gonzalez-Vega et al. (1997) have conducted a study on BancoSol, Bolivia and suggested that sources of increase in the average size of loan provide no indication that a mission drift has occurred or not. Evidence has also emerged to show that many not-for-profit MFIs have started serving the not so poor in order to maintain financial sustainability (Cull, Demirguc-Kunt and Morduch 2009).

Mission Drift in Relation to the Development of the Financial Sector

Certain problems prevailing in the credit markets, resulting from market failures, could be resolved through the actions of MFIs, which are tailor-made institutions for the purpose. In the context of the formal financial institutions serving wealthier customers, MFIs have an obligation to serve the unbanked poor. However, with the expansion of microfinance and its impact on developing economies, there is an extreme difficulty in understanding which MFIs are actually pursuing the goal of serving the poor and which MFIs have drifted away from their mission. Vanroose and D'Espallier (2013), after constructing a panel dataset with financial and outreach data of 1073 MFIs over a 10 year period, conclude that the outreach of these MFIs is satisfactory and they would be more profitable if the financial sector, where they operate, is less developed. On the other hand, a deeper level of outreach (lower average loans) has also been observed where the well-developed financial markets are present. In developed markets, the MFIs are less likely to move up market as they cannot easily compete with other established financial institutions.

Why there can be a Mission Drift?

i Granting of more individual loans

Granting of credit to individuals or entities based on their creditworthiness has been instrumental in achieving financial efficiency, in the case of commercial banks operating globally. Some MFIs, which have been influenced by the experience of commercial banks, adopt loan strategies similar to those of commercial banks, to achieve financial efficiency. Large individual loans are easy to follow-up so that there is high probability of achieving high repayment rates for such loans. However, focusing on the clients, on an individual basis, to provide banking services could result in a mission drift. Sometimes this can happen without any intention of the MFIs concerned. Having studied 124 MFIs in 49 countries, Cull, Demirguc-Kunt and Morduch (2007), show that the provision of loans, focusing on individuals is better in terms of achieving profitability. Accordingly, the growth of MFIs, their switching to wealthier customers and recording profits occur simultaneously, implying that the pursuance of sustainability and outreach simultaneously would lead to a mission drift. Cull, Demirguc-Kunt and Morduch (2009) also confirm this view and indicate that such a situation would lead to a trade-off between the outreach and commercialization objectives of MFIs.

ii Commercialization objectives

Three key elements of commercialization of microfinance are the profitability, competition and regulation, and accordingly the commercial approach seems to dominate in microfinance, as evident from the experience of Latin American countries (Christen 2000). Commercialization leads to the entry of new players and creates a competitive environment, and therefore, Christen (2000) concludes that this trend of becoming commercialized has not supported the argument that there is a mission drift. Olivare-Polanco (2005), conducting a multiple regression with data from 28 Latin American MFIs to test some of the conclusions of Christen's, indicates that certain findings of Christen are debatable. For instance, the research concludes that competition may lead to large sizes of loans and less outreach and affirms the belief that there is a trade-off between poverty outreach and sustainability owing to the commercialization of MFIs.

The commercialization of microfinance would result not only in the expansion of the individual client base, but also the increase of the share of the wealthier customers in the total customer portfolio. This trend of commercialization of MFI activities facilitates the entry of more MFIs to follow the same, eventually creating stiff competition. McIntoch and Wydick (2005) claim that increased competition among MFIs will compel some MFIs to ignore weaker customers who would become less feasible to reach. As a result, there will be more MFIs competing to increase the share of catering to the less poor. The model developed by McIntoch and Wydick further highlights that competition increases the problems of asymmetric information over creditor indebtedness and thus the loan contracts become less favorable for all borrowers. Kono and Takahashi (2009) state that the very competition among MFIs is a challenge to the microfinance industry, as rising competition might lead to lower repayment rates, as the probability of getting loans by previous defaulters increase with the presence of a large number of MFIs.

iii Lack of transparency and weak performance management

There are internal management problems that may induce a mission drift in MFIs. It has been the practice of many established commercial banks to formulate their strategic plans meticulously, possibly in consultation with experts in the field, to match the respective missions of the banks. However, in the case of most MFIs, preparation of such comprehensive plans is beyond their capabilities. Besides, the staffs in those MFIs are little informed on the targets and mechanisms by which these targets could be achieved. This results in a lack of staff performance towards achieving the mission of the institution. According to Copestake (2007, 1734), the mission drift would occur due to deeper problems of lack of transparency and weak performance management of MFIs which extend to a lack of goal setting, strategic planning, and a comprehensive client monitoring of their poverty status among others.

iv Transformation to a formal financial institution

With the informal or NGO MFIs coming under regulated financial environment, there are concerns that such MFIs may deviate from their original mission of serving the poor. This kind of transformation is sought for the realization of some perceived benefits such as the widened accessibility to commercial funding sources, wider access to potential customers, standardization and the diversification of deposit and loan products, efficiency and sustainability with the influx of capital, recruitment of qualified personnel and improvement of managerial and entrepreneurial capabilities.

However, transformation is also viewed as a risky operation, as the new structure of the MFI has to be sustained and pursued through a profit motivating drive. The application of high interest rates, favoring larger loans for customers with higher incomes would be seen as the signals of a mission drift of the transformed MFI. Haq, Hoque and Pathan (2008) suggest that prudential regulatory environment for MFIs similar to the banking sector, is useful along with the regulator's competence, supervision and enforcement skills in order to encourage the MFIs to improve outreach and attain sustainability, while protecting the depositors.

How to Avoid a Mission Drift?

If there is likelihood of a mission drift, the MFIs need to be wary of this possibility and take necessary precautions to minimize the risk of falling into a trap of this nature. One way of avoiding a mission drift is to use the services of credit agents to monitor the borrowers' profiles and activities in line with perceived targets of the MFI. These credit agents may be paid with monetary and non-monetary incentives for their task of acquiring information on potential borrowers. This exercise would be helpful in adjusting the proportion of the wealthier customers against the poor customers. However, using a theoretical paper by Aubert, Janvry and Sadoulet (2008), it has been shown that granting incentives to credit agents, although not a costly affair for pro-profit MFIs, is really a cost factor for MFIs focusing on the poor.

Managing cost for efficiency gains would ensure that sustainability remains as a feasible target. This becomes an issue for poverty focused MFIs as their staffs need to spend much time in the process of granting credit to the poor, whereas profit oriented MFIs spend comparatively lesser time in serving individual clients. The time taken to serve customers influences the cost. For instance, Tucker (2001, 111-112) mentions that the cost per loan for a first-time borrower, including the cost of attracting him or her has been between $55-$237 for Latin American MFIs. In this context, the pro-poor MFIs facing sustainability issues should not switch to serve better off-clients or increase interest rates, but rather make attempts to achieve efficiency in their operations. Using a data set of around 1000 MFIs covering the years 2006-2010, Serrano-Cinca and Gutiérrez-Nieto (2014) indicate, that in view of high operating expenses, lack of deposits and uncertain donations, the most effective strategy of avoiding a possible mission drift of an MFI would be the readjustment of its operations for better performance against the use of limited resources.

A greater role of working towards the mission objectives also lies with the employees of MFIs. The manager should educate his/her staff, working at the field level, on what is expected from them in relation to the achievement of the mission of the MFI. Sagamba, Shchetinin, and Yusupov (2013), conducted a choice experiment in Burundi to assess whether the deprived people are given preference by the loan officials of MFIs and found that the loan officers of both non-profit and for-profit MFIs had little difference in preference over the poor and they treated the social characteristics of the applicants for the loan in the same manner. The loan officials would have given preference to the poor if the managers had made them aware of their role at the field level.

REGULATIONS ON MFIs

Regulation is defined as a means of minimizing the effects of market failures. According to Chaves and Gonzalez-Vega (1992), regulation refers to a set of enforceable rules that restrict or direct the actions of participants and, as a result, changes the outcomes of such actions. In the face of intensifying competition and the changing environment in the financial sector, MFIs have diversified their activities and are actively engaged in mobilizing savings and providing other services such as insurance. The expansion of operations of MFIs has influenced certain countries to adopt more pro-active regulations covering such operations as against a laissez-faire approach followed, until recently.

A regulatory body can impose two types of regulations on financial institutions, prudential and non-prudential regulations. The prudential regulations are aimed at ensuring financial soundness, while non-prudential regulations include obligations of financial institutions towards the financial system, customers etc. The application of prudential regulations on MFIs has been studied substantially by several authors with regard to its appropriateness and effectiveness in poverty outreach (Quayes 2012, Shankar and Asher 2010; Hartarska and Nadolnyak 2007).

Benefits from Regulations

Only the regulated entities are allowed to accept deposits under existing laws in many countries. This legal clearance on the mobilization of deposits could provide the capacity enhancement of granting loans to the poor by MFIs. Flexible and less costly forms of regulations would enhance the capacity of MFIs to access long-term sources of capital at more affordable rates. On the other hand, it might also provide opportunities for the poor to improve their savings habits. The financial discipline of the clients could also be improved under a regulated regime of MFIs, as these MFIs are required to ensure that certain market principles are followed, in order to meet the regulator's requirements. On the other hand, the clients are also required to change their behavior and work under the regulated environment of MFIs. In view of this, some policy makers as well as microfinance practitioners support the view that the application of market rates of interest in the mobilization of deposits and the granting of loans is a useful way of improving client discipline in making use of the banking services.

Apart from the control of interest rates, the financial status of each MFI is closely monitored under a regulated environment. As a result, MFIs could keep an eye on their progress and foresee the cause of actions that need to be taken in order to meet the requirements of the regulator. Hence, it is argued that the impact of regulation on the sustainability of MFIs could be positive. Further, the guidance the MFIs receive from the regulator on certain other matters such as the opening of branch offices, maintenance of liquidity ratios, accounting and audit standards, restriction on managers' emoluments and various other capital requirements would be useful for the MFIs to achieve sustainability (Robinson 2001; Christen 1997).

It is suggested that, through regulations, MFIs would not only be able to achieve sustainability but also the outreach target satisfactorily. Quayes (2012), having analyzed 702 MFIs in 83 countries, showed that the average size of a loan balance per borrower for high disclosure MFIs is smaller than that of the low disclosure ones and found evidence to claim that, in the case of low disclosure MFIs, there is a trade-off between outreach and financial sustainability but for high disclosure MFIs there is a positive impact between outreach and sustainability. Also, this research asserts that the increase in the depth of outreach would also increase the profitability of high disclosure MFIs.

Moreover, regulations need to be aimed at protecting the interest of the customers as well as MFIs in a fair manner. There can be a negative impact on the sector as a whole, if such regulations are designed without taking into account country specific factors such as financial sector development and level of poverty, relevant to the country. Arun (2005), while providing a rationale for regulation in the microfinance sector anticipates that sector specific regulations along with prudential reforms, should facilitate MFIs to achieve their objectives through the capacity to mobilize savings and meet the challenges in enforcing normal banking regulations.

Are the Regulations Costly?

The regulatory body should pay attention to the fact that the cost of implementing regulations on the MFIs does not outweigh the benefits accruable from it. Some microfinance studies point out that the introduction of regulations has become an impediment to the development of the microfinance sector as a whole and has led to a mission drift (Cull and Morduch 2011; Christen and Rosenberg 2000). By analyzing 245 leading MFIs, Cull and Morduch (2011, 949) show that complying with prudential and non-prudential regulations are costly to MFIs for many reasons and, as a result, profit-oriented MFIs respond to supervision by curtailing outreach. It is further stated that as regulatory costs show the economies of scale, the average costs of smaller banks are higher than that of larger banks when they comply with regulations, while the requirement of using skilled staff in fulfilling obligations such as frequent reporting to supervisory authority could be a difficult task for smaller MFIs.

MFIs, in the fulfilment of their obligations, such as capital adequacy requirements, may switch to wealthier customers rather than the poor for the accumulation of funds. If this happens, there is a likelihood that the average size of a loan granted by MFIs would increase. In contrast, the finding of Quayes (2012) is that the average size of a loan would decrease under a regulated regime. This contention is not true as far as the operations of the MFIs in Latin American countries are concerned, according to Christen (2001) who has analyzed the impact of commercialization of some MFIs that were in operation in 18 Latin American countries. The findings of the research affirm that the regulated MFIs provide larger loans to their clients than unregulated NGOs and assert the fact that this trend of granting larger loans cannot be considered as a form of mission drift, as such an action can be a result of adopting different strategic paths in order to obtain funds and extend services to different groups of people by the MFIs.

With the introduction of regulations, some of the MFIs might need to redesign their operations and internal management to suit the monitoring requirements of the regulator. If proper changes are made by MFIs, the impact of regulations on sustainability and outreach could be managed effectively for their own benefits. However, Hartarska and Nadolnyak (2007), having studied cross country data for 114 MFIs in 62 countries, maintain that regulatory involvement has no impact on the outreach and self-sufficiency of MFIs, but indicate that better capitalized MFIs could achieve better sustainability when such MFIs are allowed to collect savings.

Rising administrative costs on lending, due to the presence of a large number of small-scale borrowers, would force MFIs to cover such costs by raising interest rates or improving the efficiency of their operations. The empirical evidence shows that the MFIs usually switch to upward interest rate adjustments, which are considered to be unhealthy in terms of outreach. As far as the objectives of policy planners are concerned, this trend needs to be curtailed for achieving poverty outreach objectives.

The use of regulations is critical in protecting the depositors and borrowers, and the financial system in general, but it could be costly to MFIs in terms of meeting the regulatory requirements, such as the submission of data and information and such costs might, therefore, outweigh the benefits under a regulated environment, according to Hardy, Holden and Prokopenko (2003).

MICROFINANCE LITERATURE ON SRI LANKA

There are certain studies that shed light on the overall microfinance operations in the country, but the discussion on the issue of sustainability versus poverty outreach focusing on a macro perspective of MFIs operating in Sri Lanka cannot be found. More specifically, available studies focus on research areas such as the improvement of the availability of information and micro credit, introduction of innovative loan products, regulatory framework and other infrastructure facilities to reach the poor, women empowerment, accessibility and affordability etc. (Premaratne 2009; Senanayake 2002).

It is necessary to provide information to general public on the availability of credit, as it would increase the customer base of MFIs (Mel, McKenzie and Woodruff 2011). They conclude in this research that access to finance by clients can be improved through product-specific financial education and also suggest that a credit registry be developed to include information about MFIs and development banks, and innovative ways of granting credit without collateral be also developed, to expand access to credit by small-scale entrepreneurs.

Tilakaratna, Wickramasinghe and Kumara (2005),[10] having conducted a sample survey consisting of 1480 households selected from 50 *Grama Niladari* divisions of 17 districts, in a study of household analysis of outreach and impact on poverty through microfinance, maintain that the main factors limiting outreach are the non-availability of infrastructure facilities and the limited opportunities available for non-agricultural activities. Their survey also identifies the availability of a wide range of microfinance providers in the country and observes that the higher unit cost of lending would occur mainly due to the extension of MFIs' operations into remote areas.

Commercialization of MFIs can be further interpreted by way of operational sufficiency, which is possible through the use of resources at a minimum level in the course of financial intermediation by them (Senanayake 2003). His research highlights that the interest rates, the role of the government and the role of donors are some critical factors that influence the commercialization of microfinance

---

[10] It has been found that the *Samurdhi* credit and savings program has been in operation in all 50 *Grama Niladari* divisions but there were no private commercial banks in operation in any of these randomly selected *Grama Niladari* divisions.

in the country. Moreover, he has also stressed the need for the marketization of both deposit mobilization and lending operations by MFIs, to achieve their commercialization objectives.

Even though the commercialization of MFIs is considered as a useful way of tackling issues relating to sustainability, this transition of MFIs could provide little benefits to the poverty stricken women headed families. Gunatilaka and De Silva (2010), using a dataset from a survey of 600 women from microfinance households in the Kurunegala District (in a study to see whether the ownership of a microfinance loan increases women's empowerment), show that with the drying up of grants, the MFIs have given more emphasis on profits and growth. Further, the research indicates that the process of commercialization of MFIs, favors the men rather than women because the enterprises managed by men are usually bigger and expandable, and have potentials to generate more returns.

In a study of the progress toward the commercialization of MFIs in Sri Lanka, Charitonenko and De Silva (2002, 2) provide details on the process of commercialization in a more different context.[11] Their study points out that the clients interviewed were in generally willing to pay non-subsidized interest rates, provided that greater and more dependable access to finance was guaranteed to them. At the same time, their study also reports that clients prefer the safety of deposits and liquidity than receiving the maximum interest rate possible on their deposits. This study further highlights that MFIs in Sri Lanka have contributed in broadening access through

---

[11] In its first phase, the administration and operation of MFIs are designed on a for-profit orientation with the development of diversified, demand-driven financial products and the application of market interest rates. In the second phase, the gradual shifting towards operational and financial self-sufficiency is pursued by MFIs through the adoption of cost recovery and cost efficiency designs and expansion of outreach. The final phase of transformation is made through the mobilization of funds using market based sources. At this stage, the MFI becomes a formal financial institution that operates on a for-profit basis under some prudential regulations and supervision, as applicable.

group formation, particularly among poor rural women. However, the weak administrative and financial controls, and widespread incorporation of social mobilization have resulted in most MFIs recording high costs, according to the study.

The rate of interest applied by MFIs in Sri Lanka is high, similar to the situation prevailing in many other developing countries. Do the MFIs in Sri Lanka in a position to adopt interest rates that are below market rates? Sanderatne (2004) contends that interest rates are not the only variable that determines viability of MFIs. It has been stated that MFIs need to balance cost and benefits while earning a small profit. Further, MFIs are unsustainable if the lending is performed at rates that do not cover the cost of funds. This article also suggests that, although cheap finance is necessary, the clientele need easy access, flexibility of repayment and financing on a multiplicity of purposes including consumption needs. Thus, sustainability depends upon operational efficiency, which includes the effective and efficient deployment of staff and their involvement in terms of the objectives of the MFI concerned.

Senanayake and Premaratne (2006) broadly indicate that the role of microfinance is important in promoting economic development in developing countries. Their research, based on the Sri Lankan experience, affirm the importance of microfinance relationship with the poor in reducing poverty, its reliance on developmental institutions which are already helping to achieve overall development, and its integration with the financial system of the country. Herath, Gunaratne and Sanderatne (2013) have also observed the positive impact of microfinance in increasing income that leads to the reduction of poverty, based on a sample of 268 households selected from the Kandy district of Sri Lanka.

On principle, MFIs are supposed to extend credit to the poor after assessing the economic viability of their projects and various other aspects of the clients, which are linked to the effective alleviation of their poverty. However, the strategies that are available with MFIs, to address the poverty of their clients through the grant of credit, can be affected by external factors that are beyond their control. Shaw (2004), having conducted a research in the Hambantota district of Sri Lanka, concludes that micro-enterprise credit is not an effective solution to alleviate poverty except for the clients who are close to the poverty line and live in conducing environments that sustain high-value microenterprises. His study also indicates that rural microenterprises serve to protect the poor and offer only limited prospects for poverty exit and the poorer clients have to face financial, cultural and geographical barriers to start occupations that generate better returns compared with clients in semi-urban areas, who can be encouraged to start higher-value occupations with any nonfinancial interventions.

There is a common belief that poverty stricken women in developing countries in general devote much of their attention on family matters, more than their male counterparts. However, when investment is externally assisted by a grant, the men report success better than women in terms of the return of the business, according to Mel, McKenzie and Woodruff (2009). Through a field level experiment conducted in Sri Lanka, they conclude that males reported profitability by investing the grant in cash or in-kind extended to them, while females were unable to use the grant to generate a sustained income. Their results show that returns to capital shocks are different according to gender differences, though the reasons for such an outcome are unexplainable.

SUMMARY

The theoretical and empirical views discussed in this chapter relate to the sustainability and poverty outreach in microfinance, the broader area of our research. Accordingly, the definitions and main features of microfinance were discussed in detail, as a precursor to other sections. Initially, the rural credit programs were implemented with the support of governments, aimed at providing finance to the poor and other deprived groups of society, at subsidized rates of interest. The theoretical basis for the implementation of such programs could be found in the supply leading finance theory. The necessity of financial liberalization, as suggested by the "McKinnon–Shaw" hypothesis, and the justification of government intervention in financial markets in developing countries, in the presence of market failures, are discussed in the context of achieving *Pareto efficiency* or a 'second best' outcome. The main purpose of the implementation of rural credit programs in achieving economic efficiency and income distribution was not successful due to widespread failures encountered in the process of implementation of these programs. The efficient allocation of resources in the rural credit markets cannot be achieved through the use of free market principles, according to some researchers.

One of the fundamental issues relevant to rural credit markets is the problem of asymmetric information. The problems of adverse selection and moral hazard occur mainly because one party (e.g. borrowers) possesses better information than the other party (eg. MFIs) when any transaction takes place between the two groups. The MFIs adopt various strategies to meet the challenges posed due to information asymmetry, including the extensive use of group lending methodology.

The role played by the money lenders in the informal sector is discussed from different viewpoints, particularly in relation to their presence on the impact of the socio-economic conditions of the poor. The rationale for the existence of dual markets in rural credit sector in developing countries is examined. Further, formal sector banks or MFIs may not supplant money lenders' role in its entirety. The formal sector favors wealthier customers, while informal lenders prefer to do business with small-scale people in the rural sector. Money lenders present in the market are important in changing the socio-economic conditions of the poor. After all, MFIs are also in a position to learn from the money lenders, especially with regard to the strategies adopted by them in reaching the poor and recovering loans. The level of interest rate prevailing in rural credit markets has been a contentious issue and therefore, it is not possible to find a theoretical basis to identify the optimal rate of interest applicable in the grant of credit to the poor.

Savings are the 'forgotten half' of microfinance. Savings provide benefits to both the borrowers and the lending institutions concerned. Borrowers may utilize the savings they have accumulated to avoid any possible default, meet future exigencies of life and collateral requirements to obtain loans and as capital for starting up their own projects. Thus, savings mobilization, serves for achieving certain objectives favorable to poor borrowers.

The presence of microfinance in credit markets in developing countries is strongly defended by the findings that it has influenced the increase of income and generation of employment among the poor communities, helped the poor to avoid seeking recourse to local money lenders, promoted gender empowerment and social solidarity and managed consumption smoothing, among other things. Nevertheless, it should also be noted that many arguments presented in favor of microfinance have been critically challenged on the basis that microfinance has failed to make a genuine and substantive economic and social impact on local communities.

The microfinance sector in Sri Lanka features, among other things; small loans to very poor people, MFIs' working in remote places, a large number of working staff of MFIs, lack of collaterals and lack of opportunities to the poor and the involvement of more women borrowers. In this backdrop, it is obvious that the views emanating from the literature on the benchmark operations of MFIs, in the maintenance of an optimal level of social commitment and financial sustainability, are diverse. There is a widely held view that focusing more on financial and institutional performance would derail the MFIs from targeting social objectives. Conversely, the overemphasis on the poor in the grant of credit may involve unmanageable costs to MFIs, resulting in inefficiency.

Although there is a vast amount of literature available on microfinance, the studies relevant to the operations of microfinance in Sri Lanka, with empirical evidence, are limited. The issue of sustainability versus outreach of the MFIs operating in Sri Lanka is merely described or evaluated in a few studies, but there has been no single, comprehensive study available on the subject. Thus, this research attempts to bridge the research gaps existing, both theoretically and empirically.

CHAPTER 3

FINANCIAL DEVELOPMENT, POVERTY REDUCTION AND MICROFINANCE - THE CASE OF SRI LANKA

INTRODUCTION

An evaluation of evolution of the financial sector and levels of poverty in the country would shed light on the linkages between finance (including microfinance) and poverty.

At the time that the country gained independence from the British in 1948, Sri Lanka was predominantly an agricultural economy, of which the major share of national income and almost over 95 percent of the country's foreign exchange earnings came from three plantation crops, tea, rubber and coconut.[12] It was a dualistic export-import economy which had been formed with a

---

[12] By 1950, the country's population had increased to 7.5 million (which was 3.5 million in 1901) and agriculture accounted for 46 percent of the GDP while the GDP per capita was estimated at USD 120 (LKR 397/-). During this time, the economy was opened to free trade. On the other hand, by 2012, the country had recorded a population of about 20 million, while the agriculture share of the GDP had come down to 11percent and the GDP per capita had increased to USD 2923 (LKR 373,001/-). Similarly, in 1950, broad money supply (M2), net foreign assets and net domestic assets were LKR 978 million, LKR 739 million and LKR 239 million, respectively, while corresponding figures for 2012 were LKR 2593 billion, LKR 112 billion and LKR 2172 billion respectively (Central Bank of Sri Lanka. 1998. *Economic Progress of Independent Sri Lanka: Published on the Occasion of the Fiftieth Anniversary of the Independence of Sri Lanka*. Colombo: Central Bank of Sri Lanka.).

fairly modern plantation export sector and a traditional, subsistence agricultural sector.

The CBSL was established in 1950 and there were only a few bank branches during this time. The money supply was managed by a Currency Board System.[13] At independence, there was a very narrow non-bank financial sector consisting of a few finance companies, and other financial institutions such as the Ceylon Savings Bank (1832), the Post Office Savings Bank (1885), the Savings Certificate Movement (1945) and Thrift and Credit Co-operative Societies (TCCSs) (1906). The emergence of the microfinance movement in Sri Lanka is linked to the TCCSs. Overall, country's financial structure in 1900s was neither complex nor developed. However, by the end of the 20th century, Sri Lanka's financial sector displayed remarkably improved features in comparison to the situation that prevailed in most of the other developing countries.

Sri Lanka maintained a 'welfare state' with free education and health, and a generous subsidy on the consumer staple, rice, which was sustained from the income generated from export earnings at the time of independence. According to the Consumer Finance and Socio-economic Survey (CFS) conducted by the Central Bank in 1953, about 40 percent of the spending units in the income ladder received only 14.5 percent of the total income of the country, whereas the richest 20 percent received 53.8 percent of the income, reflecting a considerable amount of income inequality that prevailed in the country at that time.

The socio-economic conditions and financial landscape of the country today are greatly different from those that existed in the

---

[13] The responsibility for currency issues and its management was entrusted to a Board of Commissioners, consisting of the Colonial Secretary, Treasurer and Auditor General. The Sri Lankan rupee was linked to the Indian rupee, which was considered the reserve currency of the country (Central Bank of Sri Lanka. 1998. *Economic Progress of Independent Sri Lanka: Published on the Occasion of the Fiftieth Anniversary of the Independence of Sri Lanka*. Colombo: Central Bank of Sri Lanka.).

1950s or 1960s. Social welfare programs and assets redistribution were given high priority by the state during the 1948-77 period but the post-77 period witnessed a significant reduction in government involvement in those areas. In addition, the policy makers during this period aimed at creating a small open economy. The share of national income of the poorest 40 percent of the population increased to 19.23 percent by 1973, but this share had declined, thereafter, to 16.06 percent in 1978/79, 15.25 percent in 1981/82, 14.14 percent in 1986/87 and 14.1 percent in 2003/04, according to the CFSs conducted by the CBSL[14]. The Household Income and Expenditure Surveys (HIES) conducted by the Department of Census and Statistics (DCS) in 2006/07, 2009/10 and 2016 showed that the income share of the poorest 40 percent of households had remained at low levels of 13.2 percent, 13.3 percent and 14.4, respectively. In contrast, the level of poverty, measured in terms of the Poverty Head Count (PHC) ratio,[15] had drastically reduced to 4.1 percent in 2016, from 26.7 percent in 1990/91.

In the above context, an attempt was made to explain, in an appropriate manner, the evolution of the country's financial sector and change of poverty levels with reference to microfinance, especially during the period of 1960 to 2014. The second section provides an overview of the formal financial sector development since the 1950s, while the third section explains the evolution of the MFI sector in Sri Lanka. Poverty and finance nexus - the experience of Sri Lanka is discussed in section four, in brief, while section five provides the overall conclusion of the chapter.

---

[14] CFS was not continued after it was conducted in 2003/04.

[15] The Poverty Head Count (PHC) ratio is equal to the total number of persons living under the poverty line (which is fixed at some real total expenditure per person per month during the survey period) as a percentage of the total population at national level.

AN OVERVIEW OF THE FINANCIAL SECTOR DEVELOPMENT

Economic Policy of Interest

Sri Lanka had implemented extensive social welfare programs since the 1950s until the latter part of the 1970s. It has been widely believed by some economists that the high social development achieved by the country in comparison with that of many other developing countries over the years was a result of the direct welfare provision by the state (Isenman 1980, Sen 1981, Anand and Kanbur 1991).[16] However, under the welfare state, economic growth slowed down, unemployment rate rose sharply along with the emergence of some other adverse socio-economic problems as well.[17]

The state became an important vehicle for regulating the market in which the state itself played the leading role. Internal and external trade, plantations, banking industry, telecommunications, land and land development and some of the larger industries were more or less controlled and managed by the state. According to Alailima (1986), the public sector contributed 30 percent of the GDP, more than 50 percent of total export earnings and 25 percent of total employment as at 1975. The government had spent heavily on maintaining various social welfare programs such as the subsidized rice ration scheme, free health services covering most rural areas, free education for all, and the subsidized public transport system.

---

[16] Life Expectancy: 75.0 years (2015), Literacy Rate: 93.2 percent (2015), Infant Mortality Rate: 8.5 per 1000 live births (2015), Human Development Index: 0.766 (2015).

[17] For instance, the economic growth for 1951-77 was 3.8 percent and the unemployment rate increased from 16.6 percent in 1953 to 24 percent in 1973 (Central Bank of Sri Lanka. 1998. *Economic Progress of Independent Sri Lanka: Published on the Occasion of the Fiftieth Anniversary of the Independence of Sri Lanka*. Colombo: Central Bank of Sri Lanka.).

Sri Lanka has adopted far reaching economic reforms since 1977, shifting drastically away from the hitherto maintained state dominated welfare economy. In contrast to previous economic policies, the post-77 policy package was popularly labelled as a 'growth-first, re-distribution later' drive, despite having several key programs implemented by the government to address poverty. The post-77 economic policy focused on achieving high economic growth, while keeping government intervention in economic matters at a minimum required level. The social welfare provision by the state was also gradually reduced. Further, such market oriented policy reforms also included the liberalization of financial markets and foreign trade, removal of exchange controls, promotion of private investment and the creation of employment opportunities. As a result, new jobs were created particularly with the establishment of Free Trade Zones (FTZ) and the level of unemployment fell drastically immediately after the introduction of reforms. For instance, the average annual economic growth had increased to 5.5 percent during the period of 1978-2014 compared with the 3.5 percent growth achieved during the period of 1950-1977.

The free flow of capital and labor was encouraged particularly after 1977, and as a result, the country received more foreign aid mainly for infrastructure development. A greater number of people sought foreign employment, mostly in Middle Eastern countries. The private sector participated in the key areas of economic activities such as banking, insurance, public transport, plantation management, telecommunications and construction industries. The government has been keen on investing in infrastructure development and this trend has continued on an increasing scale after the end of 30-year civil war of the country in year 2009.

The level of poverty has been on a continuous downward trend with the introduction of the policy reforms after 1977. Governments in power, having realized the link between social and political instability, and the disproportionate income distribution arising out of growth, embarked on implementing various types of welfare programs to improve the living standards of the poor. Thus, programs such as *Janasaviya* (self help), *Samurdhi* (prosperity), *Gam Udawa* (village awakening) and a variety of pro-poor credit schemes implemented with the intervention of successive governments may have contributed to recording drastic levels of poverty reduction in the country over the years. Latest data show that there has been significant poverty reduction in certain districts. For instance, districts of Colombo, Mannar and Hambantota recorded the lowest PHC ratios of 0.9, 1.0 and 1.2 respectively, by 2016.

Formal Financial Sector

The financial system of Sri Lanka has expanded over the years and financial widening (expansion of financial services and growth of financial institutions) and financial deepening (an increase of liquid money, e.g., increase of ratio of money supply to GDP or some other price index) have improved with the gradual increase of financial institutions and agents, financial instruments, regulations, transactions and market practices. Financial infrastructure, consisting of payments and settlement systems, and relevant legal framework, has also improved over the years.

The financial system of the country had been in an inactive phase until the 1950s. The establishment of the CBSL in 1950 could be considered as a turning point of its systematic expansion. At independence, there were 9 foreign commercial bank branches of British and Indian origin, accounting for nearly 60 percent of total assets of the banking sector in the country and 2 domestic banks (Bank of Ceylon and Hatton Bank Ltd.) accounting for the balance part of assets. The banking density was as low as 0.365.[18] Of the foreign banks, nearly 90 percent of the advances were in the form of overdrafts while a large part of deposits was invested abroad. The activities of the two domestic banks were basically limited to urban

---

[18] Banking density = (Number of bank offices*100,000)/Total population.

areas at the beginning of the 1950s, mostly financing short-term trading activities including export and import trade.

The demand for financial services started increasing significantly from the 1960s. During the 1960s and 1970s, the intention of the government was to localize and expand financial institutions into remote areas. The government facilitated the two state owned banks (People's Bank and Bank of Ceylon) to promote development banking, particularly for financing agricultural and industrial sectors. The two state banks gradually increased their dominance in the banking sector over foreign banks, which mainly met the financial requirements of the foreign trade sector and the working capital requirements of the plantation sector. There were a lot of administrative controls, regulations and restrictions in place, resulting in the limited scale of functioning of foreign banks. By 1970, two domestic banks accounted for 71 percent of the total deposits, 72 percent of total advances and 60 percent of the total assets of the financial institutions of the country.

The introduction of a wide range of market-oriented policy reforms since 1977 necessitated commensurate changes in the financial system. For instance, during the period of 1977-83, a total of 14 foreign banks were functioning in the country. Bank branch expansion resulted in the increase in banking density to 4.2 by 1989, thereby drastically reducing the average number of persons per commercial bank branch to 23,600. There was a greater demand for banking facilities coming from the rural poor and many banks, as a result, have responded to the growing demand by establishing more branches in rural areas.

Market forces play a key role in determining interest rates, and provide impetus for the emergence of new financial instruments and the use of technology in financial transactions. The financial sector has been further formalized with the introduction of legal, accounting and regulatory, and risk management framework for financial institutions, and along with these developments, the cost of financial intermediation has also reduced sharply. It is observed that the profit of the banking sector had recorded significant increases over the years compared with other sectors of the economy.

Table 3.1 shows that there has been a significant expansion of bank branch network of the country over the years. This has resulted in the banking density in respect of all bank branches of the country to increase from 10.6 in 1985 to 27.6 in 2014. The banking density was as low as 1.5 in the beginning of 1970s. From 1985 to 2014, domestic bank branches and foreign bank branches of commercial banks have increased by 301 percent and 784 percent, respectively, resulting in banking density of commercial bank branches to increase from 4.4 in 1985 to 13.9 in 2014. The number of branches of RDBs and CRBs that falls into the category of MFIs has increased from 930 to 2440 (or by 162 percent) from 1985 to 2014.

Table 3.1 Bank Branch Expansion during 1985 - 2014

Name of Bank	1985	1990	1995	2000	2005	2010	2011	2012	2013	2014
Commercial Bank Branches	691	745	914	1,095	1,630	2,376	2,606	2,718	2,839	2894
Domestic Bank Branches	666	722	877	1,057	1,588	2,160	2,386	2,498	2618	2673
Bank of Ceylon	327	325	339	341	388	519	560	604	624	629
People's Bank	293	308	330	343	602	679	712	726	732	732
Commercial Bank	14	19	36	81	140	190	217	229	237	241
HNB	32	40	64	120	157	198	237	239	246	244
Sampath Bank	-	13	24	39	84	172	201	204	215	224
Seylan Bank	-	17	81	90	114	124	131	147	152	162
Other[1]	-	-	3	43	103	278	328	349	412	441
Foreign Bank Branches	25	23	37	38	42	216	220	220	221	221
Regional Rural/ Regional Development Banks	16	101	171	181	212	243	248	254	255	255
NSB	56	76	96	101	130	206	213	219	219	219
Rural Banks	914	1,028	1,251	1,476	1,650	1,935	2,020	2,056	2080	2185
Other[2]	-	-	2	23	63	151	163	164	171	178
Total Bank Branches	**1,677**	**1,950**	**2,434**	**2,876**	**3,685**	**4,911**	**5,250**	**5,411**	**5564**	**5731**
Population per Bank Branch	9,444	8,714	7,450	6,421	5,331	4,205	3,975	3,757	3699	3624
Bank Branches per 100,000 Persons										
Commercial Bank Branches	**4.4**	**4.4**	**5.0**	**5.9**	**8.3**	**11.5**	**12.5**	**13.4**	**13.8**	**13.9**
All Branches	**10.6**	**11.5**	**13.4**	**15.6**	**18.8**	**23.8**	**25.2**	**26.6**	**27.0**	**27.6**

Source: Economic and Social Statistics of Sri Lanka 2015, Central Bank of Sri Lanka

[1] Includes Union Bank, Pan Asia Bank, Nations Trust Bank (NTB), National Development Bank (NDB) and Development Finance Corporation of Ceylon (DFCC) Vardhana Bank

[2] Includes DFCC Bank, Pramuka Bank, Sri Lanka Development Bank Ltd (SDBL), State Mortgage and Investment Bank (SMIB), NDB Housing Bank, Ceylinco Savings Bank and Housing Development Finance Corporation (HDFC)

According to Table 3.2, Sri Lanka had a total of 3536 bank branches as at end 2014.[19] Nearly 67 percent of all formal sector branches were located in the Western, Central, Southern and North Western provinces, which had about 65 percent of the total population of the country. The Western province, accounted for 36 percent of total branches, even though it comprised 29 percent of the total population. By the end of 2014, there were 22 domestic banks (including 09 specialized banks) and 12 branches of foreign banks operating in the country.

Table 3.2 Bank Branch Distribution by Province - 2014[a]

Province	LCBs		LSBs	Total	Percentage of Distribution
	Domestic	Foreign			
Western	947	148	159	1254	35.5
Central	290	24	67	381	10.8
Southern	295	16	108	419	11.8
North Western	190	15	63	318	9.0
North Central	154	2	55	211	6.0
Uva	143	3	44	190	5.4
Sabaragamuwa	192	9	67	268	7.6
Northern	190	2	39	231	6.5
Eastern	212	2	50	264	7.5
Total	**2663**	**221**	**652**	**3536**	**100**

Source: Central Bank of Sri Lanka

[a] Includes all commercial bank outlets except student savings units

The non-bank financial sector that includes Licensed Finance Companies (LFCs) and Specialized Leasing Companies (SLCs) had expanded, accounting for 7.1 percent of the total assets of the financial sector during 2014. Total loans and advances had increased to LKR 604 billion in 2014 from LKR 521 billion in 2013. As at end 2014, there were 46 LFCs and 7 SLCs under the supervisory

---

[19] However, with the number of CRBs (2185) and students savings units of commercial bank branches, the number of bank branches had increased to 6591 as at end 2014.

and regulatory purview of the CBSL. According to Table 3.3, of the 1132 branches of these non-bank financial institutions, nearly 65 percent were located in the Western, Central, Southern and North Western provinces.

Table 3.3 Branch Distribution of LFCs/SLCs by Province - 2014

Province	Number of Branches	Percentage of Distribution
Western	369	32.6
Central	128	11.3
Southern	125	11.0
North Western	118	10.4
North Central	86	7.6
Uva	60	5.3
Sabaragamuwa	83	7.3
Northern	75	6.6
Eastern	88	7.8
Total	**1132**	**100**

Source: Central Bank of Sri Lanka

Table 3.4 reveals the amount of assets of financial institutions and private sector credit growth in relation to the GDP for the period of 1960 to 2014. Accordingly, the total assets of the financial system and credit to the private sector had been increasing during the said period. The total assets of financial institutions with respect to the GDP had increased from 43 percent in 1960 to 115 percent in 2014. A substantial part of the increase of total assets of financial institutions is accounted for by the increase in the asset base of the Employees' Provident Fund (EPF). The increases in assets of other institutions, such as insurance companies and finance companies, have also contributed to the increase in assets in the financial sector.

The private sector credit by commercial banks to nominal GDP as a percentage is a useful indicator in measuring the financial development of a country. According to Table 3.4, this ratio had significantly increased over the years and reached the highest level of 41.5 percent in 2012, but had declined slightly to 38.1 percent in 2014. It is evident from Table 3.4 that the financial institutions, while increasing their assets, had also extended credits to the private sector over the years. It can be observed that the private sector investment has increased substantially starting from the 1980s, as a result of the easing of many investor bottlenecks under liberalized economic policies.

Table 3.4 Assets of Financial Institutions and Private Sector Credit 1960 - 2014

Year	Assets of Commercial Banks (LKR Bn)	Total Assets of All Financial Institutions (LKR Bn)	Assets of All Financial Institutions as a Percentage of GDP	Credit to Private Sector (LKR Bn)	Credit as a Percentage of GDP
1960	1.10	2.90	42.70	0.50	7.30
1965	1.60	5.10	67.10	0.70	9.20
1970	2.70	8.80	64.20	1.60	11.70
1975	4.40	12.70	47.40	3.40	12.70
1980	22.20	67.70	102.10	11.40	17.20
1985	54.90	171.90	105.90	33.60	20.70
1990	115.90	357.70	111.10	63.10	19.60
1995	328.60	880.30	131.90	207.50	31.10
2000	597.90	1,459.30	115.90	362.60	28.80
2005	1,257.10	2,979.40	121.50	806.90	32.90
2006	1,536.30	3,462.00	117.90	998.30	34.00
2007	1,822.40	4,311.20	120.60	1,190.10	33.30
2008	1,963.10	4,790.40	108.50	1,276.60	28.90
2009	2,230.30	5,053.00	104.50	1,529.10	31.60
2010	2,566.70	6,578.60	117.40	1,896.90	33.90
2011	3,157.70	7,712.30	117.90	2,587.50	39.50
2012	3,757.40	8,837.80	116.20	3,146.70	41.50

| 2013 | 4,328.30 | 10,318.30 | 118.90 | 3,595.50 | 37.50 |
| 2014 | 4,855.90 | 12,041.00 | 115.00 | 3,983.00 | 38.10 |

Source: International Financial Statistics
Central Bank of Sri Lanka

Data in Table 3.5 show that the financial sector in Sri Lanka reflects a range of new developments that has taken place over the years and has the institutional elements of a growing financial system. According to Table 3.5, the commercial banks, two of which are state-owned, dominate in terms of assets, accounting for 48.9 percent of the total assets. LFCs have expanded their activities recently, yet they possess only about a 6.5 percent share of total assets of the financial system. Institutions not regulated by the CBSL represent about 21.3 percent of assets of the total assets, of which the EPF accounts for 12.3 percent. Rural Banks and TCCSs, together, have only a share of 1 percent of the total assets of the financial system.

Table 3.5 A Classification of Assets by Financial Institutions - 2014

Name	Total Assets (LKR Bn)	Percentage of Total Assets
The Central Bank of Sri Lanka	1464.3	12.2
Institutions Regulated by the Central Bank	8,016.4	66.6
Deposit Taking Institutions	7,751.7	64.4
Licensed Commercial Banks	5,884.6	48.9
Licensed Specialized Banks	1,087.5	9
Licensed Finance Companies	779.6	6.5
Other Financial Institutions	264.7	2.2
Primary Dealers	191.1	1.6
Specialized Leasing Companies	73.6	0.6
Institutions not Regulated by the Central Bank	2,560.7	21.3
Deposit Taking Institutions	112.4	0.9
Rural Banks *(a)*	103.5	0.9
Thrift and Credit Co-operative Societies *(a)*	8.9	0.1

Contractual Savings Institutions	2,272.9	18.9
Employees' Provident Fund	1,486.9	12.3
Employees' Trust Fund	199.1	1.7
Approved Private Provident Funds *(b)*	134.2	1.1
Public Service Provident Fund	41.0	0.3
Insurance Companies *(c)*	411.7	3.4
Other Financial Institutions	175.5	1.5
Stock Broking Companies *(d)*	11.3	0.1
Unit Trusts/ Unit Trust Management Companies*(d)*	128.6	1.1
Market Intermediaries* *(d)(e)*	29.6	0.2
Credit Rating Agencies *(d)*	0.3	0
Venture Capital Companies	6.2	0.1
Total Assets	**12,041.4**	**100**

Source: Central Bank of Sri Lanka

(a) Registered with the Department of Co-operative Development

(b) Registered with the Department of Labor (c) Regulated
by the Insurance Board of Sri Lanka

(d) Regulated by the Securities and Exchange Commission of Sri Lanka

(e) Market Intermediaries include Underwriters, Margin Providers and Investment Managers

* Excluding the assets of Licensed Banks, LFCs and SLCs
which are registered as Market Intermediaries

Commercial banks are active virtually in all aspects of financial services, with some of them having subsidiaries or affiliates engaged in insurance and capital market activities. A variety of other institutions, such as merchant banks, leasing companies, unit trusts, credit rating agencies, venture capital companies and foreign currency banking units, operate with the active participation of the private sector, while catering to the various financial needs of the people. The provision of financial services is supported further with the extensive use of technology, particularly by the commercial banks.

The financial system of the country has evolved into key distinguishable areas, such as money market, bond market, foreign exchange market and the equity market. The inter-bank call money market, which is also a part of the money market in the formal banking system, facilitates commercial banks to manage their liquidity positions through the lending and borrowing among banks. The gross transaction volume of call money in 2014 stood at LKR 2,198 billion per day, while the daily weighted average call money rate varied between 5.29 percent and 7.02 percent during 2014. The volatility of call money rates could be controlled through the open market operations of the CBSL. Further, the inter-bank foreign exchange market facilitates the determination of the exchange rate of the Sri Lankan Rupee under a free floating mechanism. The total volume of inter-bank foreign exchange transactions stood at US$ 15.48 billion in 2014.

In the government securities market, the Treasury bills are the most liquid and substantially traded instrument. By end 2014, the outstanding stock of Treasury bills and Treasury bonds amounted to LKR 694.8 billion and LKR 2,844.1 billion, respectively, while the total volume of Treasury bills valued at LKR 2,243.3 billion and Treasury bonds valued at LKR 760 billion were transacted on an outright basis during the same year.

The commercial paper (CP) market has shown some improvement with the issuance of CPs to the value of LKR 8.2 billion during 2014 with the support of banks. Further, the country's debt securities market was also able to raise LKR 54.2 billion through 20 debenture issuances in 2014. The increased involvement of private sector in CP issuance and debt issuance in the recent past could be attributable to the credit restrictions imposed on banks by the CBSL and the relatively high lending rates charged by banks and finance companies.

In the Colombo Stock Exchange (CSE), market intermediation has developed with the market capitalization of the CSE amounting to LKR 3,104.8 billion while representing about 29.7 percent of the GDP as at the end of 2014. The All Share Price Index (ASPI) was increased by 4.7 percent, and the S&P Sri Lanka 20 Index, based on the performance of the 20 largest blue chip companies listed in the CSE was also increased by 25.3 percent in 2014 compared with the previous year.

Presently, Sri Lanka has also introduced innovative payments and settlement systems. The Real Time Gross Settlement (RTGS) system in the LankaSettle System, operated by the CBSL, facilitated 85 percent of the total value of non-cash payments of large value relating to the call money market, the government securities market, open market operations and the time critical settlements of the country during 2014. The value of payments settled through the RTGS amounted to LKR 59,551 billion in 2014. The Check Imaging and Truncation (CIT) system, operated by LankaClear (Pvt.) Ltd., cleared over 49.0 million Checks amounting to LKR 8.4 billion during 2014. The Sri Lanka Interbank Payment System (SLIPS), has assisted in the speedy settlement of transactions through credit cards, debit cards etc. under an improved real time settlement platform. There were 3,341 Automated Teller Machines (ATMs) and 34,904 Electronic Fund Transfer Facilities at Point of Sale Machines (EFTPOS) in the country by the end of 2014. The credit cards in use by the end 2014 were estimated to be 1,032,833. The legal framework governing financial issues has also been developed in tandem with other changes taking place in the financial system.

Informal Sector

Informal sector financing in Sri Lanka has been investigated and evaluated by some researchers, but in comparison with the data availability on formal sector financing, data on the informal sector remain limited. Overall, the informal sector has facilitated the savings, borrowing and investment of unbanked people, even though money lenders' services always come under criticism for different reasons including the charging of high interest rates from the borrower. However, it is widely accepted that informal lending is less cumbersome and devoid of rigid rules on the borrower although his/her liability to the lender remains high in comparison with the liability that would have been created if he/she had opted to borrow from the formal sector.

Some useful information is available in the CFSs conducted by the CBSL with regard to the size of informal sector lending and the replacement of informal lending by formal sector lending over the years from the 1960s. In 1963, only about 7.6 percent of loans in Sri Lanka had been from the formal sector, but nearly 40 years after this survey, i.e., in 2003, this share had increased to 45 percent, representing 61 percent of total value of loans. Over the years, informal institutions including money lenders has been playing a dominating role as shown by Table 3.6.

Table 3.6 Loans Granted by Formal and Informal Institutions

Year Type of Institution		1963	1973	1978/ 79	1981/ 82	1986/ 87	1996/ 97	2003/ 04
Formal Institutions	**Number as a Percentage**	7.6	11.5	10.7	9.7	16.6	43.1	45
Informal Institutions		92.4	88.5	89.3	90.3	83.4	56.9	55
Formal Institutions	**Value as a Percentage**	n.a.	n.a.	25.3	38	39.8	67.3	61.1
Informal Institutions		n.a.	n.a.	74.7	62	60.2	32.7	38.9

Source: Consumer Finance and Socio-economic Survey
(various issues) Central Bank of Sri Lanka

n.a.: Not available

According to Sanderatne (1982), non-institutional sources of credit continued to be perhaps the more dominant source of credit to small farmers, despite several improvements that had been made in the provision of institutional credit in Sri Lanka. Informal credits are granted at very high rates of interest for certain cases and Sanderatne mentions that one third of informal credit was interest free, over 10 percent of credit was fixed at interest rates of 15 percent, about 12 percent of credit was fixed at interest rates over 50 percent and less than 1 percent of credit was above 150 percent, per annum. Further, Sanderatne states that over 70 percent of informal lending was provided for production purposes while 10 percent of fund was provided for the trading sector during the 1970s and 1980s. He also reports that most of the informal sector lending was given without obtaining any collateral by the lender.

Table 3.7 Distribution of Loans by Type of Security

Type of Security	Number as a Percentage		Amount as a Percentage	
	1996/97	2003/04	1996/97	2003/04
No Security	57.8	54.5	35.5	37.7
Personal Guarantee	6.7	9.9	10.4	20.8
Immovable Property	1.6	1.2	30.6	9.1
Jewelry/Consumer Durables	31.2	31.0	11.9	20.8
Other	2.7	3.4	11.6	11.6
Total	**100**	**100**	**100**	**100**

Source: Consumer Finance and Socio-economic Survey (various issues)
Central Bank of Sri Lanka

Table 3.7 indicates that where both the number of loans and volume of loans are concerned, the informal sector finance without collateral is significantly higher. This fact implies that one of the prime reasons to seek loans from the informal sector is the borrowers' ability to obtain loans without any pledge being given to the lender in the form of assets, which, however could be impossible if credit is sought from the formal sector.

There is no official estimate on the current status of informal sector finance. An island-wide survey of microfinance institutions commissioned by the GTZ ProMiS (Promotion of the Microfinance Sector) program in 2006/2007 (Czura 2010)[20] records that 32 percent

---

[20] This impact assessment uses cross-sectional data from a household survey of over 760 client households from all regions in Sri Lanka, to evaluate the impact of the initial ProMiS program phase (September 2005 - November 2009) on microfinance clients. For this purpose, five MFIs that had received technical assistance from ProMiS during a given period had been selected.

of MFI members have sought credit from the informal sector during the survey period. The Microfinance Industry Report (2009)[21] estimates that only 18.3 percent households have borrowed from informal sources such as moneylenders, family, friends, neighbors, traders, landlords, and Rotating Savings and Credit Associations (ROSCAS/Seettu).[22] Further, it has been found that the use of informal credit in the estate sector (20.8 percent) is slightly higher than the average of informal credit from all sectors and substantially higher than that of the urban sector (16.6 percent).

Further, the Microfinance Industry Report of 2009 affirms that the main reason for borrowing from informal sources relates to the meeting of emergency needs in the case of 45 percent of the number of loans, or 22 percent of the value of the loan. This survey also observed that 75 percent of people had indicated that the principal reason for accessing informal credit was the easy access/the ability to borrow money quickly, whereas 67 percent had cited the reason for the same as the lack of collateral requirements. Overall, it can be concluded that the share of informal sector lending in comparison with total lending in the country has gradually decreased, implying that the branch expansion of commercial banks as well as development banks such as RDB, SANASA, and CRBs at regional levels could have been instrumental in bringing about such results.

MICROFINANCE SECTOR IN SRI LANKA

Historical Development in Brief

In Sri Lanka, microfinance has been introduced for the purpose of serving the underprivileged community with the establishment

---

[21] A report produced by GTZ-ProMis.

[22] Under ROSCAs, a group of individuals agrees to start a common fund for which a regular cyclical contribution is required to be made by each member ensuring a lump sum amount for each member on a rotational basis.

of TCCSs in the early years of the 20th century, under the then colonial administration of the British. During this period, there were around 3.6 million people in the country and the economy was predominantly centered on agriculture while there were a significant number of people engaged in trade and other business activities. The main role of TCCSs at that time was to procure inputs for farming activities and distribute them among needy people. These TCCSs were taken over by the Consumer Co-operative Societies established in the 1940s, which were renamed for some reasons as Multipurpose Co-operative Societies in the 1950s.

By the late 1970s, the number of TCCSs in operation came down drastically, but they were reorganized and revived under a new name, SANASA. There were also CRBs that came under Multipurpose Co-operative Societies. SANASA and CRBs came under the purview of the DCD. TCCSs are registered under the Co-operative Societies Law No. 5 of 1972. TCCSs and CRBs have extended their services to the poor over the years and have transformed into more structured entities at present.

The year 1985 saw a new development initiative in the field of microfinance with the arrival of Regional Rural Development Banks (RRDBs), which gradually evolved to 17 banks over the years, with the geographical coverage of entire country. In the 1980s, the socio-economic condition of Sri Lanka was very different from the today. For instance, during 1980, agriculture contributed as much as 28 percent of the GDP, the rate of poverty in terms of the PHC ratio was as high as 30 percent and the country had only about 950 bank branches. In this background, setting up of RRDBs was an initiative to expand credit to the rural poor in order for them to engage in agricultural activities and other cottage industries, with a view of spurring growth and generating more employment opportunities in rural areas.

In the early phase of its development, RRDBs adopted a poverty lending approach and nearly 80 percent of their loans were granted to the poorest segments of the population. The restructuring and recapitalization of RRDBs took place in 1998-1999 and simultaneously, 17 RRDBs were brought under six Regional Development Banks (RDBs). Later, all six RDBs were brought under one national level body (Pradeshiya Sanwardhana Bank or Regional Development Bank), which presently operates focusing on achieving financial sustainability. The RDB had made LKR 1.4 billion profit before tax and had recorded a deposit portfolio of LKR 72.52 billion and a loan portfolio of LKR 61.0 billion as at end 2014.

With the adoption of liberalized economic policies, a number of NGOs and commercial banks have also entered into the microfinance business. The government introduced the *Janasaviya* program in 1989, aimed at alleviating poverty, and this program was replaced by the *Samurdhi* development program in 1995. By 2012, this program covered about 2.6 million people through 1050 *SBSs* that were established island-wide. The short-term strategy of the *Samurdhi* program includes sub-components for income support, social insurance and social developments, which are essential parts of any poverty cushioning approach. On the other hand, the long term strategies focus on poverty reduction under a program of social mobilization, empowerment and integrated rural development. Beneficiaries have been facilitated to start income generating activities with loans provided through *Samurdhi* banks. A compulsory savings component would indirectly improve financial engagements of the beneficiaries.

The National Development Trust Fund (NDTF) established in 1991 as an apex lending institution was also involved significantly in the microfinance sector in Sri Lanka. The governments in recent years have also implemented various other poverty alleviation programs such as *Gemi Diriya*, *Gama Neguma* and *Divi Neguma* with a built-in-micro credit component. Under *Divi Neguma*, the successor to the *Samurdhi* program, there were about 3.6 million members in community banking unions established island-wide as at end 2014.

The CBSL, in the past, has implemented various subsidized credit schemes and refinance schemes to support needy sectors and people. For instance, the CBSL introduced a medium and long term credit fund (MLCF) as far back as 1964, to provide credit at concessionary rates to medium scale enterprises. The commercial banks were provided the credit at rates ranging between 3.0 percent - 6.0 percent per annum while the end customer rate was fixed below 8 percent per annum. There was a remarkable interest from commercial banks to grant credit under the scheme. Further, the CBSL also took steps to introduce a new agricultural credit scheme in 1967, in order to provide finance facilities to agricultural farmers under concessionary rates of interest.

Providing finance facilities to the poor through the intervention of the governments in power continued even after private sector entry into the banking industry, which has increased substantially since 1977. Further, a rural credit advisory board was established in 1981 in order to liaise banking sector activities to support government policies for the development of the rural sector. Accordingly, credit facilities were channeled to the rural poor under various concessionary credit schemes, enabling them to engage in and develop agricultural, fisheries, industrial and other self-employment activities.

Even during recent years, the CBSL, with the financial support received from the government and other external organizations, has implemented several credit schemes specially designed for the purpose of alleviating poverty among people. These micro finance projects focus on financing income generating activities of the poor. During the year 2012 alone, about 10,100 beneficiaries had been granted loans to the value of LKR 652 million to commence income generating activities under the poverty alleviation micro-finance project II (PAMP II), which operated in 14 districts in the country. Two other projects, the poverty alleviation microfinance project - revolving fund loan scheme and small farmer and landless credit project - revolving fund (SFLCP-RF) loan scheme, disbursed LKR 387 million among 9,612 beneficiaries and LKR 180 million among 5,704 beneficiaries, respectively, to commence income generating activities during 2012. Of the total loan amount of the two schemes, 46 percent was disbursed for trading and other services while 19 percent, 15 percent and 13 percent were given to small industries, livestock and agriculture, respectively. By the end of 2015, microfinance loans extended with the involvement of the CBSL amounted to LKR 2139.5 million in respect of 34,385 beneficiaries. In the meantime, the small holder plantation entrepreneurship development program provided financial assistance to marginalized small holders in selected divisional secretariat divisions in the districts of Kandy, Kegalle and Nuwara-eliya and upland food crop farmers in the intermediate zone of the Monaragala district. Further, the dry zone livelihood support and partnership program focused on improving the livelihood of farmers in the districts of Anuradhapura, Badulla, Monaragala and Kurunegala with the disbursement of microfinance loans under the self help group (SHG) system.

Further, the CBSL took steps to establish its first Regional Office (RO), at Matara in 1981. Thereafter, in 1982 and 1985, two ROO were established at Anuradhapura and Matale, respectively. It was 25 years later, i.e., in 2010, that another two ROO were set up at Jaffna (presently located at Killinochchi) and Trincomalee. At the time of the first branch office of the CBSL that was established at Matara in 1981, socio-economic conditions of the country were remarkably different from what we can witness today. For instance, in the 1980s, banking was a service beyond the reach of the majority of micro and small-scale entrepreneurs in rural areas. There was a need to finance the poor under the concessionary credit schemes and facilitate them to gain technical knowhow in order to start business ventures. In these initiatives, it was anticipated of creating a conducive environment to promote balanced regional development. Chandrasiri (2008) indicates that successive governments during post-liberalization have recognized regional industrialization as an important policy option and some of the steps taken in this direction include the strengthening of the regional industry services committee, assistance for the preparation of feasibility reports, establishment of industrial estates and facilitating the access of technology.

Establishment of branch offices in the 1980's by the CBSL has resulted in facilitating the provision of banking services to the rural mass and promoting banking habits among them. Further, the ROO have been engaging in the implementation of the main functions of the CBSL and other development activities at a regional level, in terms of the Monetary Law Act of 1949 as amended, and under the guidance of the CBSL management. Accordingly, during the 1980s and 1990s, the ROO were involved in granting loans under several credit schemes operated through the then Rural Credit Department of the CBSL and conducting *'Janahamuwas'* (meetings at village level) with a view of improving financial literacy among the poor. In addition, the ROO were also engaged in providing other facilities such as check clearing, currency operations and investment in government securities in the respective regions.

The CBSL, through its five ROO established at Matara, Anuradhapura, Matale, Jaffna and Trincomalee, has facilitated micro, small and medium sector entrepreneurs (MSMEs) to obtain loans to engage in viable economic activities. During 2012, the ROO had also conducted 155 skill development programs on subject areas such as scientific farming practices, post-harvest techniques, high-tech agriculture, and best practices in medium and small-scale projects including agriculture, in association with the relevant institutions in the respective provinces. In addition, many other awareness programs had been conducted by the ROO during 2012, on various development related subjects.

Table 3.8 Programs Conducted by the ROO of the CBSL - 2012

Regional Office	Awareness Programs		Skill Development Programs	
	Number of Programs	Number of Participants	Number of Programs	Number of Participants
Southern Province	84	6,606	37	1,032
North Central Province	89	7,707	38	1,378

Central Province	107	6,966	31	1,044
Northern Province	114	8,530	17	569
Eastern Province	75	6,846	32	1,361
Total	**469**	**36,655**	**155**	**5,384**

Source: Central Bank of Sri Lanka

Many international and local NGOs and several commercial banks have entered into the field of microfinance particularly after the 1990s using different microfinance models. Commercial Banks have taken some initiatives to provide microfinance loans and it is observed that the Hatton National Bank's (HNB) *Gami Pubuduwa* (village awakening), started in 1989, has been an instrumental factor for other commercial banks to enter into microfinance. The *Gami Pubuduwa*, which delivers banking facilities with affordability, also promotes the accessibility of finance to the non-bankable population based on equality and meritocracy, devoid of discrimination (HNB PLC, Annual Report - 2008). Bank of Ceylon, People's Bank as well as Commercial Bank PLC also actively participate in microfinance activities at present.

Current Status

i Client outreach and loan and deposit portfolio

Sri Lanka has a microfinance sector served by a diverse range of institutions, as shown in Table 3.9.

Table 3.9 Key Indicators of Operations of MFIs in Sri Lanka - 2014

Type of Institution	No of Branches	Client Outreach (Loans/ Membership)	Loan Portfolio (LKR Mn)	Deposits (LKR Mn)	Source
TCCSs and SANASA Societies	8,724[1]	902,132[1]	4,575[1]	5,687[1]	CBSL, LMFPA

NGOs/Limited Liability Companies/ Companies Limited by Guarantee	2,500	1,000,000	n.a.	n.a.	2006/2007 GTZ ProMiS Survey
CRBs and Women's Development Co-operatives	2,185	1,505,176	37,757	89,634	CBSL
Samurdhi Bank Societies (SBSs)	1,340[1]	2,588,059[1]	84,251[1]	47,098[1]	http://www. Samurdhi. gov. lk, MOF
Pradeshiya Sanwardhana Bank (PSB/RDB)	265	788,081	63,571	72,059	CBSL, LMFPA
SANASA Development Bank PLC (SDBL)	82	379,218	33,080	40,573	CBSL, MOF, LMFPA
Licensed Finance Companies (LFCs)	12	364,539	19,521	n.a.	CBSL
Licensed Commercial Banks (LCBs)	4	943,000	65,224[2]	n.a.	2006/2007 GTZ ProMiS Survey, CBSL
Total	**15,112**	**8,470,205**[3]	**307,979**	**255,051**	

LMFPA - Lanka Microfinance Practitioners' Association

MOF- Ministry of Finance

[1] As at end 2012

[2] Loan portfolio with each loan less than LKR 2 million

[3] Based on number of loan accounts except for SBSs where number of members are taken into account

n.a.: Not available

The GTZ ProMiS (Promotion of the Microfinance Sector) survey in 2006/2007 showed that at least 10,000 MFI outlets were active across the country during the survey period. According to the CGAP CLEAR Review (2006), there had been about 14,000 providers of microfinance in Sri Lanka during the survey period.[23] As Table 3.9 shows, 15,112 branch outlets of MFIs including their head offices had engaged in microfinance as at end 2014. These MFIs accounted for nearly 9.3 percent of the total value of loans granted by commercial banks in the country as at end 2014.

ii Geographical distribution

Table 3.10 Geographical Distribution of MFIs in Sri Lanka

Province	Percentage of MFIs[1]	Percentage of PTCCSs & CRBs[2]
Western	12.2	17
Central	10.1	10
Southern	24.0	16
North Western	10.2	15
North Central	3.9	5
Uva	10.8	7
Sabaragamuwa	11.2	9
Northern	5.2	14
Eastern	12.3	7

Source: [1] **GTZ-ProMiS Survey 2006/07**
[2] **Microfinance Review- Sri Lanka, Analysis and Performance Report 2012**

The regional distribution of MFIs based on the 7141 MFI outlets that participated in the GTZ-ProMiS Survey of 2006/07 (RDBs, SBSs and 3794 active societies of SANASA, 85 percent of CRBs and 83 NGO-MFIs, all representing 70 percent of total outlets of MFIs in Sri Lanka) and SANASA Primary Thrift and Credit Co-operative Societies (PTCCSs) together with Co-operative Rural Banks (CRBs) are given in Table 3.10.

---

[23] This number includes the network of SANASA societies of 8,440, although, more than 50% of them were inactive at that time suggesting further that the active number of MFIs that existed in the country during survey period were close to 10,000.

Table 3.10 shows that the Southern province had the highest number of MFI outlets whereas the North Central province had the lowest number of MFI outlets. Similarly, the Western and North Central provinces had the highest and lowest number of PTCCSs & CRBs, respectively. The information revealed by Table 3.10 is useful to analyze further, the correlation between the number of MFIs and the level of poverty prevailing by province, which, however, is not possible within the scope of this research.

iii Regulatory framework applicable to MFIs

It appears that there is no coherent policy for the supervision and registration of MFIs in Sri Lanka. NGO MFIs are mostly registered as social service organizations under the Voluntary Social Service Organizations (Registration and Supervision) Act, No. 31 of 1980. Some of the Guarantee Limited Companies and Private Limited Finance Companies are registered under the Companies Act, No. 7 of 2007. Several finance companies engaged in microfinance activities are registered under the Finance and Leasing Act, No. 56 of 2000 and Finance Companies Act, No. 78 of 1988.

A large number of NGOs that are involved in microfinance have self-control mechanisms and in some cases, they are subjected to supervision by their parent companies. NGOs with religious or social welfare objectives operating in the country, have become the least supervised entities. The SBSs, CRBs, TCCSs, RDB, SDBL and other licensed banks involved in microfinance, fall under respective supervisory mechanisms which have already been described in the first chapter of this book.

Meanwhile, a regulatory and supervisory framework was introduced for MFIs in Sri Lanka, with the enactment of Microfinance Act, No. 6 of 2016 in May 2016. Accordingly, no person other than a licensed MFI or an exempted entity can carry on microfinance business. However, banks licensed under the Banking Act, No. 30

of 1988, finance companies licensed under the Finance Business Act, No. 42 of 2011 and community-based organizations established with social objectives and engaged in microfinance business are not subject to supervisory mechanism proposed under the Microfinance Act.

The authority set up by the CBSL is responsible for licensing/ registering, regulating and supervising companies, NGOs, co-operative societies and societies that are registered under the Companies Act, No. 7 of 2007 or Voluntary Social Service Organizations (Registration and Supervision) Act, No. 31 of 1980, to carry on microfinance business. The monetary board of the CBSL is vested with the power to implement policies and procedures in maintaining standards on regulation and supervision of microfinance business in the country.

iv Other salient features of the microfinance sector

The GTZ-ProMiS Survey 2006/07 is a useful reference to understand other aspects of MFI operations in the country.

Table 3.11 Other Salient Features of MFIs

Description	Status
Informal credit as a Percentage of credit received from MFIs	25
Percentage of MFI outlets by sector	
Rural	89.4
Urban	9.6
Estate	1.0
Average size of a deposit (LKR)	
Rural	46,274/-
Urban	21,245/-
Estate	9,972/-
Average size of a loan (LKR)	84,000/-
Percentage of MFI members who sought credit from informal sector	32

Purpose of borrowing (Percentage)	
Agriculture	18.8
Business/Enterprise	16.7
Construction/Housing	28.8
Assets/Durables	8.0
Consumption	3.3
Emergencies	16.7
Settlement of loans	4.1
Other	3.6

Source: GTZ-ProMiS Survey 2006/07

It can be observed from Table 3.11 that informal credit to credit received from MFIs during the survey period stood at 1: 3. This is a reflection that informal lending plays a key role in meeting borrowing requirements of the rural poor. Further, Table 3.11 also reveals that nearly 65 percent of the total loans obtained by MFI borrowers were utilized for non-income generating activities such as construction of houses and purchase of assets. Further, the Table shows that the average size of a deposit in the estate sector is very small, reflecting the low level of income received by the workers of the estate sector. The average size of a loan of LKR 84,000/- reported in 2006/07 also reflects the size and nature of projects for which the loans had been obtained. It is evident that the size of an average deposit is significantly smaller in comparison with the size of a loan.

The GTZ-ProMiS Survey 2006/07 also showed that the average size of a savings account was LKR 36,763/-, and 91.6 percent of total clients had opened savings accounts. About 28.6 percent of the clients had even obtained different types of insurance schemes such as life insurance, health insurance and accident insurance. In summary, the study shows the overall improvement of household businesses due to microfinance. The survey also showed that 59.1 percent of the borrowers had obtained individual loans while 40.9 percent of the borrowers had obtained group loans. About 80.5 percent of borrowers had benefitted in working with the groups, according to the survey. On the other hand, this indicates that customers do not receive full benefits they expect from MFIs, if they interact with MFIs individually.

According to the Microfinance Review-Sri Lanka, Analysis and Performance Report 2012,[24] the average size of microfinance loans differs by type of MFI as shown in Table 3.12. It is a noteworthy feature that the average size of loan per borrower in co-operatives is the highest, while companies and NGOs record low average sizes of loans.

Table 3.12 Average Size of Microfinance Loans by Type of MFIs - 2012

Type of Institution	Average Loan Balance (LKR)
LSBs	50,675
NBFIs	23,649
Co-operatives	63,817
Companies	20,816
NGOs	22,189
Average of All Institutions	**36,229**

Source: Microfinance Review - Sri Lanka, Performance and Analysis Report- 2012

Table 3.12 further indicates that, overall average size of a loan granted by MFIs in Sri Lanka stood only at LKR 36,229/- as at end 2012. However, the average size of an SME loan granted by banking sector in Sri Lanka was around LKR 260,000/- as at end 2012 (Annual Report- 2012, Ministry of Finance and Planning) whereas the corresponding average loan size in respect of commercial bank lending could have been significantly higher than that of MFIs.

---

[24] Lanka Microfinance Practitioners' Association, 2012, *Microfinance Review - Sri Lanka, Performance and Analysis Report-2012*, Rathnayaka Enterprises, Rajagiriya.

POVERTY AND FINANCE NEXUS - SRI LANKAN EXPERIENCE

Poverty and Inequality Trend

PHC ratio of Sri Lanka came down drastically from 26.7 percent in 1990/91 to 8.9 percent in 2009/10, 6.7 percent in 2012/13 and 4.1 percent in 2016.[25] as shown in Table 3.13. As evident from the data of the Table, along with the decline in poverty levels in urban and rural sectors over the years, a remarkable drop of poverty in the estate sector is also noticeable, although the estate sector poverty decrease was subject to certain variations at times due to changes in relative prices of food items as well as employment and wages in the estate sector since 2006/07, according to DCS.

Table 3.13 Poverty Head Count Ratio of Sri Lanka by Sector

Sector/Sri Lanka	Poverty Head Count Ratio in the Years of						
	1990/91	1995/96	2002	2006/07	2009/10	2012/13	2016
Urban	16.3	14.0	7.9	6.7	5.3	2.4	1.9
Rural	29.5	30.9	24.7	15.7	9.4	7.5	4.3
Estate	20.5	38.4	30.0	32.0	11.4	6.2	8.8
Sri Lanka	**26.1**	**28.8**	**22.7**	**15.2**	**8.9**	**6.5**	**4.1**

Source: Household Income and Expenditure Surveys
Department of Census and Statistics

The significant improvement in the reduction of poverty in Sri Lanka qualifies the country for achieving the millennium

---

[25] The PHC ratio is equal to the total number of persons living under the poverty line during the survey period as a percentage of the total population at national level. The DCS declared that the official poverty line was LKR 4,166 per person per month - or LKR 139 per day in respect of the year 2016. The level of income was derived using the absolute poverty line approach. In other words, this amount of money is needed for an average person to meet the cost of his/her basic needs, which include the cost of food, clothing, housing, education, transport, and medicine.

development goal of halving poverty by 2015. Further, with regard to poverty at district levels, by 2016, poverty as measured by the PHC ratio has decreased considerably in some districts such as Colombo (0.9 percent), Gampaha (2.0 percent), Hambantota (1.2 percent), Mannar (1.0 percent) and Vavuniya (2.0 percent) while it still remains high in certain other districts such as Mullaitivu (12.7 percent), Killinochchi (18.2 percent), Batticaloa (11.3 percent) and Trincomalee (10.0 percent). Interestingly, certain districts with higher rates of poverty also have a low density of financial institutions and weak financial inclusiveness.

Table 3.14 Poverty Head Count Ratio of Sri Lanka by District

District	Survey Period							No. of Poor Persons 2016
	1990/91	1995/96	2002/03	2006/07	2009/10	2012/13	2016	
Colombo	16.2	12.0	6.4	5.4	3.6	1.4	0.9	19,790
Gampaha	14.7	14.1	10.7	8.7	3.9	2.1	2.0	45,827
Kalutara	32.3	29.5	20.0	13.0	6.0	3.1	2.9	35,719
Kandy	35.9	36.7	24.9	17.0	10.3	6.2	5.5	76,429
Matale	28.7	41.9	29.6	18.9	11.4	7.8	3.9	19,357
Nuwara Eliya	20.1	32.1	22.6	33.8	7.6	6.6	6.3	46,257
Galle	29.7	31.6	25.8	13.7	10.3	9.9	2.9	30,775
Matara	29.2	35.0	27.5	14.7	11.2	7.1	4.4	36,544
Hambantota	32.4	31.0	32.2	12.7	6.9	4.9	1.2	7,450
Jaffna	n.a.	n.a.	n.a.	n.a.	16.1	8.3	7.7	46,052
Mannar	n.a.	n.a.	n.a.	n.a.	n.a.	20.1	1.0	1,005
Vavuniya	n.a.	n.a.	n.a.	n.a.	2.3	3.4	2.0	3,526
Mullaitivu	n.a.	n.a.	n.a.	n.a.	n.a.	28.8	12.7	12,003
Kilinochchi	n.a.	n.a.	n.a.	n.a.	n.a.	12.7	18.2	21,249
Batticaloa	n.a.	n.a.	n.a.	10.7	20.3	19.4	11.3	60,912
Ampara	n.a.	n.a.	n.a.	10.9	11.8	5.4	2.6	17,431
Trincomalee	n.a.	n.a.	n.a.	n.a.	11.7	9.0	10.0	39,718
Kurunegala	27.2	26.2	25.4	15.4	11.7	6.5	2.9	47,930

Puttalam	22.3	31.1	31.3	13.1	10.5	5.1	2.1	16,708
Anuradhapura	24.4	27.0	20.4	14.9	5.7	7.6	3.8	33,140
Polonnaruwa	24.9	20.1	23.7	12.7	5.8	6.7	2.2	9,051
Badulla	31.0	41.0	37.3	23.7	13.3	12.3	6.8	56,698
Monaragala	33.7	56.2	37.2	33.2	14.5	20.8	5.8	27,187
Rathnapura	30.8	46.4	34.4	26.6	10.4	10.4	6.5	72,715
Kagalle	31.2	36.3	32.5	21.1	10.8	6.7	7.1	60,435

Source: Household Income and Expenditure Surveys
Department of Census and Statistics

The Poverty Gap Index (PGI) measures the depth of poverty in a country or region (based on the aggregate poverty shortfall of the people in poverty relative to the official poverty line) while Squared Poverty Gap Index (SPGI) measures the severity of the poverty of people who are poor (it gives more weight to people living in lower category of poverty). Six districts which have relatively higher depth of poverty in terms of PGI are Kilinochchi, Mullaitivu, Batticaloa, Trincomalee, Rathnapura and Kegalle while the same districts are found to be having more severity of poverty, in terms of SPGI, according to Table 3.15.

Table 3.15 Poverty Gap Index and Squared Poverty Gap Index -2016

District	PGI	SPGI
Colombo	0.2	0.1
Gampaha	0.3	0.1
Kalutara	0.4	0.1
Kandy	1.0	0.2
Matale	0.6	0.1
Nuwara Eliya	0.8	0.2
Galle	0.4	0.1
Matara	0.5	0.1
Hambantota	0.1	0.0
Jaffna	0.9	0.2
Mannar	0.1	0.0
Vavuniya	0.2	0.1

Mullaitivu	2.1	0.5
Kilinochchi	3.4	1.0
Batticaloa	1.8	0.5
Ampara	0.4	0.1
Trincomalee	1.8	0.5
Kurunegala	0.4	0.1
Puttalam	0.3	0.1
Anuradhapura	0.5	0.1
Polonnaruwa	0.5	0.2
Badulla	0.7	0.1
Monaragala	0.7	0.1
Rathnapura	1.1	0.3
Kagalle	1.1	0.3

Source: Household Income and Expenditure Survey-2016
Department of Census and Statistics

The HIES surveys of DCS show that Sri Lanka is yet to achieve considerable progress in reducing economic inequality among its people. Table 3.16 provides the Gini Coefficient for each of the categories of household income, per capita income, and income receivers' income for 2016 and indicates further that inequality persists in the provinces and remains high in the Western, Northern, North Western, North Central and Uva provinces compared with other provinces in terms of income receivers' income.

Table 3.16   Income Inequality by Province and Sector - 2016

Province	GINI Coefficient of		
	Mean Household Income	Per Capita Income	Income Receivers' Income
Western	0.45	0.45	0.51
Central	0.42	0.41	0.49
Southern	0.42	0.40	0.49
Northern	0.44	0.41	0.52
Eastern	0.42	0.40	0.46
North Western	0.46	0.44	0.53

North Central	0.46	0.45	0.53
Uva	0.45	0.42	0.50
Sabaragamuwa	0.41	0.39	0.47
Sector			
Urban	0.48	0.48	0.53
Rural	0.44	0.42	0.50
Estate	0.36	0.34	0.42
Sri Lanka	**0.45**	**0.44**	**0.51**

Source: Household Income and Expenditure Surveys
Department of Census and Statistics

Although poverty is measured predominantly in terms of the level of consumption, expenditure or income, it includes multi-dimensional aspects such as education, health, infrastructure, employment, housing, land ownership etc. There are differences by districts and provinces with regard to the non-income poverty levels.

According to the Human Development Index (HDI), an alternative measurement of poverty and deprivation of the population of a country compiled by the United Nations Development Program, Sri Lanka stood at the 73rd place (0.766) out of 188 countries in 2015, ahead of other South Asian countries. The HDI value of Sri Lanka in 2015 shows a significant increase of 22.4 percent compared with the HDI value in 1990 which was 0.626.

Poverty Levels Versus Breadth of Finance

There is a gradual expansion of bank branch network in the country by districts, observable through higher banking density as shown in Figure 3.1. It also implies a positive relationship between the expansion of branches and poverty reduction in the country.

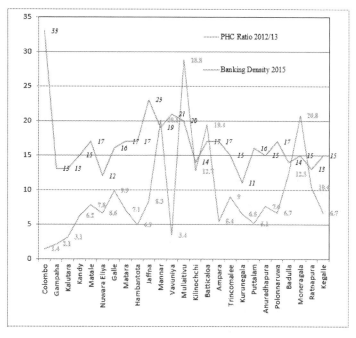

**Figure 3.1 Poverty Head Count Ratio (2012/13) and
Banking Density (2015) by District**
Source: Central Bank of Sri Lanka

According to the graph (Figure 3.1), the comparison of PHC ratio and banking density by district shows that the gap between these two variables is very large in the districts of Colombo, Vavuniya, Hambantota and Jaffna, just because these districts possess high density of banking and/or low PHC ratio. The districts of Ampara, Puttalam, Anuradhapura and Pollonnaruwa also record significant gaps implying that the presence of bank branches has been a favorable factor in the determination of the PHC ratio of each district.

The Southern province, having almost one fourth of MFIs, records a banking density of 16, 17 and 17 in 2014 for the three districts representing Galle, Matara and Hambantota respectively, while the PHC ratios of those three districts in 2012/13 were 9.9, 7.1 and 4.9, respectively. Considering the behavior of banking density and PHC ratios of the districts, there is no evidence to presume that the MFIs presence in terms of branches represents any relationship with the breadth of formal financial institutions or the levels of poverty prevailing in those districts. On the other hand, the Eastern province that includes the districts of Ampara, Batticaloa and Trincomalee and also the Uva province representing the districts of Badulla and Moneragala have different incidence of poverty, a fairly high density of bank branches and also the presence of a large number of MFIs.

The district-wise data available on banking density and PHC ratios for 2016 plotted in Figure 3.2 indicates a relationship between these two variables, similar to the relationship shown in Figure 3.1, except for some variations relating to few districts.

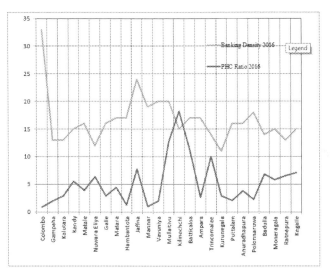

Figure 3.2 Poverty Head Count Ratio and Banking Density by District- 2016
Source: Central Bank of Sri Lanka

It is evident from Table 3.17 that respective GDP shares of provinces had recorded slight increases during the period of 2007 to 2016, except for Western and Southern provinces.

Although, it is important to identify the trend of increase of the GDP as against the increase of financial institutions including MFIs in the provinces, there is no justification to pursue the objective of examining causal relationship between such variables based on raw data presently available for this study.

Table 3.17 GDP Shares by Province 2007-2016

Year / Province	2007	2011	2012	2013	2014	2015	2016
Western	46.5	44.4	42.8	42.5	41.6	39.9	39.7
Central	9.6	9.8	10.2	10.5	10.4	10.6	10.5
Southern	10.5	11.1	11.0	10.4	10.9	10.1	10.1
Northern	2.9	3.7	3.7	3.5	3.6	4.1	4.2
Eastern	5.2	5.7	6.3	5.9	6.0	5.7	5.7
North Western	9.9	10.0	10.0	10.5	10.7	10.6	10.7
North Central	4.0	4.6	5.0	5.0	5.1	5.9	5.8
Uva	4.9	4.5	4.8	4.9	5.0	5.6	5.8
Sabaragamuwa	6.4	6.2	6.2	6.8	6.7	7.5	7.5

Source: Central Bank of Sri Lanka

Despite the increase of the GDP shares of the provinces other than Western and Southern provinces over the years, Table 3.18 shows that the GDP contribution in terms of persons in Western province is significantly higher in comparison with that of other provinces.

Table 3.18 Provincial GDP Share Weighed According to Provincial Population[a]

Year / Province	2007	2011	2012	2013	2014	2015	2016
Western	0.000812	0.000750	0.00730	0.00721	0.00701	0.00667	0.00659
Central	0.000368	0.000360	0.00395	0.00403	0.00395	0.00399	0.00390
Southern	0.000434	0.000441	0.00443	0.00415	0.00430	0.00395	0.00391
Northern	0.000258	0.000308	0.00347	0.00326	0.00332	0.00375	0.00379

Eastern	0.000348	0.000366	0.00404	0.00375	0.00377	0.00353	0.00347
North Western	0.000433	0.000423	0.00419	0.00437	0.00441	0.00433	0.00432
North Central	0.000335	0.000367	0.00393	0.00389	0.00393	0.00450	0.00436
Uva	0.000383	0.000335	0.00378	0.00381	0.00384	0.00426	0.00435
Sabaragamuwa	0.000336	0.000316	0.00320	0.00349	0.00340	0.00377	0.00373

[a] **(Provincial GDP Share/Provincial Population) *100**
Source: Calculated by the Author

SUMMARY

Economists, more often, find that there is a positive correlation between economic growth and financial sector development. The financial sector development takes place with the development of a wide array of institutions, instruments and markets but the contribution from MFIs within this broader framework is considered to be marginal. This is conspicuous when taking into consideration of MFIs' ability in mobilizing and allocating resources compared with that of other formal sector financial institutions of an economy. However, MFIs have been recognized as a key player in providing financial facilities to certain disadvantaged sections of the population, in order for them to engage in micro level economic activities. In this context, it is necessary to evaluate the financial sector performance and poverty trends of Sri Lanka over a few decades and review the magnitude of operations of MFIs in reaching the poor in the past within the broader framework of the financial system of the country.

It has been highlighted in this chapter that from 1960 to 1977, Sri Lanka had implemented economic policies that brought little or no-competition among market players in the financial sector. The weak financial intermediation by commercial banks and strong government intervention in the financial sector activities during this period had been financially repressive. However, during the post-77 period, the financial sector was gradually opened up and as a result, a significant number of foreign and local banks came into operation in the country. As evident by the data given in Table 3.5, since 1977, the country's financial sector has considerably expanded in terms of asset creation, resulting mainly from the grant of credit to the private sector. However, Sri Lanka cannot claim to have a broad and vibrant financial sector particularly in comparison with the market activities taking place and availability of money and capital market instruments in many other active financial markets of the world.[26]

There have been some empirical investigations of the impact of financial development on poverty reduction. Accordingly, it is believed that, up to a threshold level of economic development, the financial sector growth helps to reduce poverty through the growth enhancing effect, but this relationship may not persist due to any change in income inequality resulting from the same financial development. Reduction of poverty in Sri Lanka is substantial as evident from the drastic decrease in the PHC ratio over the years. This level of change in poverty would have occurred along with the implementation of some massive poverty alleviation schemes in the country. At the same time, there has been an increase in MFIs' presence in the Sri Lankan financial sector and, arguably, there would have been some positive impact on improving the economic conditions of the poor through the services offered by these institutions as well. Several micro level studies that have been carried out to assess the impact of MFIs on the poverty reduction of the country also point out the presence of a healthy relationship between these two variables.

However, it has been observed that certain poverty alleviation programs such as *Samurdhi* has not been properly targeted towards the poor in the country since its inception. According to the World Bank, in the year 2000, almost 40 percent of households ranked in the lowest expenditure quintile were missed out, while many

---

[26] A long-term corporate bond market is virtually absent in the country although about LKR 54.2 billion worth of debentures were issued through initial public offerings (IPOs) in 2014. The value of the debentures issued through IPOs in 2016 was LKR 78 billion.

not so poor families received consumption grants and other forms of benefits. It has been identified that political interference in the selection of beneficiaries and corrupt practices of some officers have adversely affected the overall success of this program.

In conclusion, it can be stated that evaluation of the depth and breadth of Sri Lanka's financial system and its evolution from the 1960s to 2014 and linking its behavior to changing poverty levels with reference to microfinance operations of the country was very useful to further evolve this study. Besides, we also observe that poverty levels of the country have reduced along with the financial sector development including the expansion of MFIs in the country. Nevertheless, through these relationships, it is not possible to discern the impact of operations of microfinance on the change of poverty levels of the country, which however, is not an objective of this research.

CHAPTER 4

A BRIEF DISCUSSION ON ANALYTICAL FRAMEWORK

INTRODUCTION

The trade-off that can possibly exist between financial sustainability and the depth of outreach is known as 'mission drift'. As discussed in chapter 1, several studies have found that a mission drift does not or cannot occur under certain given conditions. Thus, the identification of such conditions under which MFIs are able to achieve profitability and the depth of outreach in tandem is important to the overall focus of this study. It was noted that there is a strong argument for the unattainability of a 'win-win' situation for MFIs when they focus on catering to the absolute poor. Similarly, it has also been pointed out that the outreach objectives could be achieved along with financial performance, if MFIs can effectively manage their strategies particularly in relation to credit delivery, pricing of products and the allocation of resources among others.

The profitability of a firm is strongly related to its product competitiveness and market share, both of which are a function of innovation by the firm. Hence, the innovative approaches adopted by MFIs should also lead to the improvement of the depth of the market of MFIs. For instance, attractive lending products at affordable costs to the clients would be a key driver in increasing market penetration. However, an MFI could also exercise its discretion to adopt a strategy by which it could limit its access to the poorest of the poor and emphasize on high-end clients in order to achieve financial performance. In this study, attention has been paid to comprehend whether MFIs' attempt to seek profits overshadows their objective of serving the poor. The second section of this chapter focuses on the key areas of poverty outreach and financial sustainability in the analytical framework with a schematic representation. In the third section, the hypotheses of the research have been elaborated. The remainder of the chapter deals mainly with sub-topics such as sample selection, research designs and methods and the rationale for the selection of variables.

KEY AREAS UNDER REVIEW IN THE ANALYTICAL FRAMEWORK

Certain key areas under review in this book require elaboration and understanding in the context of the hypotheses formulated within the analytical framework. Poverty in a broader sense is multi-dimensional, with income fulfilling the task of meeting basic needs while human, physical, environmental, social, political resources along with property rights serve as a means of receiving income. Poverty is also expressed in multi-dimensional outcomes, manifested by conditions relating to food and shelter, health, nutrition, human and political rights and shaped by socio-economic, cultural, institutional and political environments (Zeller 2003). On the other hand, financial sustainability with regard to MFIs is defined as the ability of these institutions to cover the cost of money lent, out of the income generated from the loan portfolio and to reduce operational costs to minimum possible levels (Hermes and Lensink 2011).

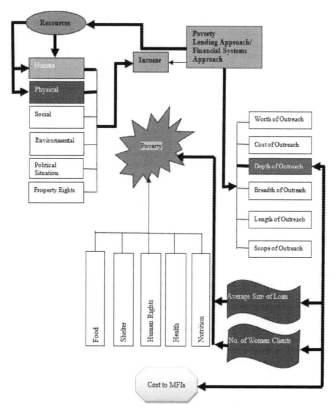

Figure 4.1 MFI Operations in Changing the Poverty Status
Source: Created by Author based on Hermes and Lensink (2011);
Zeller (2003); Schreiner (2002); and Robinson (2001)

The analytical framework of this research is shown in a
schematic form in figure 4.1. Schreiner (2002) presents six aspects
of microfinance outreach. They are described in terms of worth,
cost, depth (proxies are the number of women customers, size of
loans, location, education, ethnicity and housing), breadth (number
of clients), length (time frame of supply of microfinance) and scope
(types of financial contracts finalized) of outreach. Accordingly,
depth of outreach is the value that society places to the net gain of
a given client. Schreiner (2002, 594) substantiates this by stating
that – "direct measurement of depth through income or wealth

is difficult. Simple, indirect proxies for depth are sex (women are preferred). The most common proxy for depth is loan size."

According to Robinson (2001), the poverty lending approach of MFIs focuses on addressing poverty through the facilitation to increase physical and human capital of the poor. According to her view, the average loan size of the poor should lie below the average loan size of economically active poor or people who are at the threshold of exiting poverty level as the capacity of the poor to repay loans and MFIs' willingness to provide credit at low costs to such borrowers pull the loan size downward. On the other hand, Hermes, Lensink and Meesters (2011), using data from 435 MFIs for the period of 1997-2007, show that there is a trade-off between sustainability and outreach. They have measured sustainability through the cost efficiency of MFIs and the depth of outreach through the average loan balance and percentage of women borrowers. In a nutshell, there would be positive changes of the outcome variables described by Zeller (2003) through direct intervention by MFIs in the form of providing small loans, particularly targeting more women clients.

This study mainly focuses on examination of financial outcomes of MFIs in relation to their pursuing of depth of outreach. In this context, Figure 4.1 shows the broader framework, based on which the research questions are structured and developed further resulting in other main components of the research such as the formulation of hypotheses, analysis of data and the presentation of the implications and conclusions.

FORMULATION OF HYPOTHESES

Figure 4.1 shows that the two variables, average size of loan and the number of women clients, which are used as proxies to measure the depth of outreach can be linked to the cost variable of an MFI. The administrative costs on client identification, follow-up of projects and related paper work as a ratio to the loan size decreases when the loan size increases, provided that other factors affecting the said cost items remain normal. Further, the general consensus in the credit market is that the smaller the size of the loan, greater the probability that the loan goes into the hands of a marginal borrower.

As highlighted in the literature survey chapter, women clients have been identified as an effective mean to address the outcome variables of poverty (food, shelter, health, nutrition etc.), which are also depicted in Figure 4.1. Extending credit to women clients and its relationship to cost of the MFI could be realistically measured through a composite index representing the proportion of women participation in the loan portfolio and the size of loans. When these aspects are considered and linked to MFIs' operations, a valid question could be raised; whether MFIs that are pursuing to achieve depth of outreach can also be successful in managing the cost and achieving financial sustainability. The main reason of raising this question is that the poverty lending approach of MFIs could cause their overall cost to rise. MFIs have many options to counter this problem of rising cost particularly through the adoption of different lending schemes to improve recoveries and achieve cost efficiency. In this background, another valid question could be raised; whether the type of lending operations carried out by an MFI differently affects its poverty outreach and financial sustainability.

On the basis of the research questions already identified, we could formulate some hypotheses (alternative) as described below:

HYPOTHESIS 1

> H_1: If an MFI's operational sustainability increases, then the average size of its loans decreases (There is a positive relationship between financial sustainability and depth of outreach which is measured in terms of the average size of loans).

It has been argued that the granting of small loans carries an additional workload for any financial institution in terms of monitoring, supervision, record keeping, documentation etc. Despite these costly affairs, MFIs have proven that they could maintain high recovery rates and cost efficiency, which are essential to earn adequate profits and overall sustainability.

HYPOTHESIS 2

H_1: If an MFI's operational sustainability increases, then the composite index of the average size of its loans, plus percentage of males obtaining loans decreases (There is a positive relationship between financial sustainability and depth of outreach which is measured in terms of average size of loans and the share of females obtaining loans).

It has been accepted that the granting of loans to women borrowers would be useful in expanding the poverty outreach of MFIs, but this would require the financial institutions to carry additional costs in servicing the loans that are of small sizes. Despite the cost involved, MFIs have proven that they could maintain high recovery rates and cost efficiency when they grant loans to women clients, resulting in sound financial performance.

HYPOTHESIS 3

H_1: If an MFI implements GLSs more than individual lending schemes, then the poverty outreach of the said MFI will also increase.

It is assumed that the group loan schemes are conducive for achieving poverty outreach in contrast to the individual loan schemes, which may have an opposite impact on poverty outreach.

Under the group concept, the individuals with lack of capacities particularly in terms of their income levels and submission of required collaterals are organized in to groups. Usually, the average value of loans granted to a group member is lower than the average value of loans granted to an individual not organized in to a group.

HYPOTHESIS 4

H_1: If an MFI is operationally self-sufficient, then poverty outreach of the said MFI remains positive.

The viewpoint to be tested in the above context is whether MFIs that are financially self-sufficient can make a positive impact on poverty outreach as opposed to MFIs that are not financially self-sufficient. When MFIs can cover financial cost, operating cost and provision for loan impairment from their income, such MFIs could achieve self-sufficiency thereby facilitating these MFIs to extend their operations to more and more disadvantaged groups.

HYPOTHESIS 5

H_1: If the size of the assets of an MFI increases, then poverty outreach of the said MFI will also increase.

While liabilities such as equity and debt capital, can be translated into asset items in the balance sheet of an MFI, the prudential use of assets to generate the income of an MFI comes mainly from the grant of loans. Assuming that the loans portfolio correlates positively with the poverty outreach, the overall impact of assets which include other liquid and fixed assets is assumed to be positively correlated with poverty outreach.

HYPOTHESIS 6

$H_{1:}$ If an MFI increases the number of female loan officers,
then poverty outreach of the said MFI will also increase.

According to the alternative hypothesis, it is believed that female loan officers possess the capacity in accessing more female clients than their male counterparts. Besides, the project monitoring and guidance available to female clients through female loans officers would help record better recovery rate of loans for MFIs, inducing MFIs in turn to extend more loans to women. This situation is assumed to help in establishing positive relationship between female loan officers and poverty outreach of an MFI.

HYPOTHESIS 7

$H_{1:}$ If an MFI increases the number of its branches, then
poverty outreach of the said MFI will also increase.

It is believed that having more branches would impact on the overall cost of operations of an MFI to rise, compelling it to scale up the granting of loans. At the same time, MFIs should take into account the necessity to establish branches in areas where disadvantaged groups can be served better. In such circumstances, employees would be able to maintain a close relationship with the clients, which would ultimately help to achieve better recovery rates and cost efficiency for MFIs.

HYPOTHESIS 8

$H_{1:}$ If an MFI implements GLSs more than individual
lending schemes, then the said MFI will also be able to
achieve sustainability.

It is assumed under H_1 that the group loans are conducive for achieving sustainability of MFIs. Under the group system, individuals with lack of creditworthiness who are grouped together may be granted loans, but cost efficiency along with the high recovery rates of such loans would also ensure that MFIs achieve the sustainability as well.

SELECTION OF THE SAMPLE

Firstly, the analysis of sustainability and poverty outreach by the MFIs in Sri Lanka has to be carried out after selecting a sample of MFIs based on their mandates/missions and activities. If the mandate/mission explicitly states that a particular MFI has been pursuing solely one objective, i.e., either a financial performance objective or poverty outreach objective, such MFI has not been included in the sample.

Secondly, the MFIs selected for the sample are those that report or provide their financial data at least to one of the data sources of this research i.e., Microfinance Information eXchange (MIX) Market, Lanka Microfinance Practitioners' Association, or the CBSL. Accordingly, data are collected from Microfinance Information eXchange (MIX) Market, MIX Market Information Platform and the MicroBanking Bulletin (MBB), which is a publication of the MIX Market, publications of Lanka Microfinance Practitioners' Association, World Development Indicators of the World Bank and the publications of the CBSL.

Thirdly, a purposive sampling method was used in the selection of the sample, which was finalized taking into account the mandate/mission of each category of MFIs concerned. The work context of certain types of MFIs in relation to their respective mandates is briefly reviewed below for this purpose.

SCREENING MFIs FOR THE INCLUSION IN THE SAMPLE

Data available in Tables 3.9, 3.10, 3.11 and 3.12 show that microfinance in Sri Lanka has expanded in terms of its scale and spatial outreach in recent years with the presence of a large number of different types of MFIs. These MFIs adopt a variety of approaches in lending and providing other services to meet small borrower needs, guided by their respective mandates/missions. Irrespective of having certain differences in terms of mandates, the MFIs under review have also shown unique features that are common to their lending operations.

Thrift and Credit Co-operative Societies (TCCSs)

TCCSs are the oldest microfinance providers in Sri Lanka. They were re-organized into a federation under the SANASA banner during the late 1970s. Most of the TCCSs in the Northern province operate as independent institutions from the SANASA movement. Both SANASA TCCSs and other TCCSs are registered with and supervised by the DCD. These TCCSs grant loans from the savings they mobilize in addition to the loan funds obtained from the SDBL. The Federation of Thrift and Credit Co-operative Societies of Sri Lanka, as the umbrella organization of primary societies dealing in microfinance, has a vision to establish *'new social order based on co-operative principles and values'*. Each TCCS enjoys a certain degree of independence to governance, but is required to follow the co-operative philosophy and the bottom-up management style. It is obvious that they operate under a one to one close relationship built up with the clients based on social ethics rather than financial principles. In view of the mandate of TCCSs, they were not considered for the sample.

MFIs Registered as NGOs/Companies

It has been estimated that there are about 2500 local and international NGOs engaged in microfinance activities in the country but only about 50 of such MFIs could be ranked as having a satisfactory asset base, geographical coverage and financial soundness (Atapattu 2006; Lanka Microfinance Practitioners' Association 2012; Mix Market 2012). The NGO MFIs are registered under the Social Services Organization (registration and supervision) Act, No 31 of 1980 as amended, while companies are registered under Companies Act, No 7 of 2007. The financial data for a majority of NGOs are not available for public scrutiny resulting in difficulties to figure out how financial controls are applied or how efforts are made to reach the poor by such MFIs.

Although, NGO MFIs are not permitted to mobilize deposits, in practice many such MFIs implement certain schemes that are virtually capable of mobilizing deposits in various forms. On the basis of the availability of data and mandates of operations, certain MFIs registered as NGOs/companies have been selected for the sample.

Co-operative Rural Banks (CRBs)

The first CRB was set up in 1964 to provide small loans to rural households for the purpose of meeting their specific needs. The activities of CRBs are more approachable, people oriented and therefore more attractive to small-scale clients compared with commercial banks (Charitonenko and De Silva 2002). Achieving financial efficiency has not been focused on and prioritized by the CRBs.

Over 2500 CRBs coming under Multi-Purpose Co-operative Societies (MPCSs) and owned by their members are registered and supervised by the DCD. Profits earned by a well-functioning CRB could be transferred to a parent MPCS that has financial difficulties. Most of these institutions do not commit for effective financial management let alone profit maximization. Therefore, the study of the relationship between financial efficiency and outreach of these institutions may not be fruitful in the context of our research.

Samurdhi Bank Societies (SBSs)

Samurdhi Bank Societies (SBSs) came into existence in 1996, as part of the National *Samurdhi* Program that was implemented throughout the country aimed at alleviating poverty within extreme poverty groups. There were 1040 SBSs in the country by end 2012, providing financial assistance to approximately 2.6 million people. The projects financed by SBSs are comparatively small in financial volumes while such projects often target community development aspects of underprivileged people.

There are no proper regulations applicable to the supervision of SBSs. The government subsidizes these Banks and they are often criticized of being politically vulnerable. It is said that the support extended by the government would be both the cause and result of the widespread inefficiencies prevailing in SBSs. Further, the lending approaches of these institutions are not strictly restrictive on the use of funds. Considering the fact that the sustainability of SBSs depends upon the support extended by the government, the SBSs have been excluded from the sample.

Pradeshiya Sanwardhana Bank (Regional Development Bank)

The year 1985 marked the arrival of a new development bank with microfinance focus, namely the RRDBs, now known as the RDB. RRDBs came under the direct control and supervision of the CBSL in its early phase of development.

The restructuring and recapitalization of RRDBs took place during 1998-1999 and simultaneously 17 RRDBs were brought under six RDBs, namely Rajarata Development Bank, Ruhuna Development Bank, Wayamba Development Bank, Uva Development Bank, Kandurata Development Bank and Sabaragamuwa Development Bank. Later, all six RDBs were brought under one national level body in May 2010, designated as the Pradheshiya Sanwardana Bank (PSB or Regional Development Bank/RDB) and established as a statutory body under the Pradheshiya Sanwardana Bank Act, No. 41 of 2008. The PSB presently operates relying more on commercial principles (However, the average size of a loan is small compared with that of commercial banks. For instance, in 2012, the average size of a loan of the RDB was LKR 71,033/-), although their operations during initial years were based on the 'barefoot banking concept'.

Sanasa Development Bank PLC (SDBL)

The SDBL is a limited liability company incorporated in Sri Lanka on August 06, 1997. It was re-registered under the Companies Act, No. 7 of 2007 on October 30, 2007. The SDBL functions as the main credit institution for the SANASA movement. A majority stake in the SDBL is collectively held by SANASA societies. Its operations are linked to co-operative movement to a certain extent with the provision of credit to the rural poor. It also provides technical assistance, entrepreneurial skills and information technology assistance to the people, and promotes collective business enterprises in rural communities. The average size of a loan of the SDBL is small compared with that of commercial banks (for instance in 2012, the average size of a loan was LKR 52,702/-). Thus, the SDBL is an institution that has an interest in reaching the poor particularly in rural communities while achieving its own financial sustainability.

Non-Bank Financial Institutions (NBFIs)

The latest entrants to the microfinance field are the RFCs, which are registered under the Finance Business Act, No. 42 of 2011 that had replaced the Finance Companies Act, No. 78 of 1988. The Department of Supervision of Non-Bank Financial Institutions (DSNBFIs) of the Central Bank is entrusted with the regulatory and supervisory functions in respect of LFCs, for the purpose of ensuring that the RFCs comply with the minimum prudential requirements stipulated by the CBSL.

The RFCs are subject to off-site surveillance and on-site examinations by the DSNBFIs. Further, the directions and rules issued under the provision of the Finance Business Act address, inter alia, the minimum capital adequacy and liquidity requirements, provisioning for bad and doubtful debts, single borrower limits, and limits on equity investments of RFCs. Microfinance is carried out by some RFCs with a special concurrence given by the CBSL, but the overall mandate of RFCs is to achieve their profit maximization objective through normal operations. The selection of RFCs to the sample would expand the types of MFIs covered while also improving the level of confidence on the results of hypotheses tested. Accordingly, five RFCs significantly engaged in microfinance were selected for the sample.

Licensed Commercial Banks (LCBs)

It has been observed that commercial banks such as the government owned People's Bank (PB), Bank of Ceylon (BOC) and privately owned Hatton National Bank PLC. and Commercial Bank of Ceylon PLC. have entered into microfinance operations and continued the same to some extent. These banks have granted loans less than LKR 2 million each, amounting to a total of LKR million 7,394 by end 2014.

As a whole, commercial banks have recently taken initiatives to extend micro credit as part of fulfilling their corporate social responsibility. However, no separate financial information in respect of microfinance loan portfolios is available with banks and therefore, there is no possibility of incorporating these data/banks in our sample. Besides, microfinance loans by these banks represented only 3.7 percent of the total loan portfolio of all banks in the country in 2014.

RESEARCH DESIGN AND METHOD - MODEL I

Research questions of this study are addressed through the use of two different types of research methods. Model I was developed in relation to the main hypothesis of the first research question of this study; whether one could accept or reject the claim that emphasis on financial sustainability by an MFI has any negative impact on its poverty outreach.

Description of Variables

Table 4.1 Variable Description - Model I

Variable Name	Label	Description
Outreach 1 (Dependent)	ALBL	Log of average loan balance per borrower
Outreach 2 (Dependent)	ALMBL	Log of average loan balance per borrower plus percentage of male borrowers
Branch Network	NOO	Number of branches in operations including head office
MFI Size	ASTL	Log of total assets ('000)
Cost per Borrower	CPB	Total expense/Number of active borrowers
Female Loan Officers	FLOs	Number of female loan officers
Gross Loan Balance	GLBL	Log of gross loan balance ('000)
Operational Self-Sufficiency	OSS	Operating revenue/ (Financial expense + Operating expense + Provision for loan impairment)
Total Expense Ratio	TER	(Financial expense + Operating expense + Write-off amount)/Assets
Women Borrowers	WBR	Number of women borrowers/Total number of borrowers

Dummy Variables		
Group-based Lending	LGD	1 if MFI implements group lending vigorously and zero otherwise
Individual-based Lending	LID	1 if MFI implements individual lending vigorously and 0 otherwise
Dummy OSS	OSSD	1 if Firm is Financially Self-Sufficient (i.e. OSS>=100 percent) and 0 otherwise
Interaction Variables		
Log of OSS x Group	OSSG	Log of OSS x LGD (interaction of OSS and group lending)
Log of OSS x Individual	OSSI	Log of OSS x LID (interaction of OSS and individual lending)

Source: Based on Quayes (2012), Kumar Kar (unpub.) and Cull, Demirguc-Kunt, and Morduch (2007), CGAP (Consultative Group to Assist the Poorest) (2003)

Determination of Dependent and Independent Variables

The models used in the research have been developed on the basis of similar models that have been adopted by Quayes (2012), Kumar Kar (unpub.) and Cull, Demirguc-Kunt, and Morduch (2007). Accordingly, the basis of selection of the dependent and independent variables of the regressions involving hypotheses one to seven (1-7) is explained below.

i Dependent variable as the average loan balance per borrower

It is assumed in our benchmark regression that if MFIs grant more smaller size loans which could even be smaller than the prevailing average loan size in the credit market, the poor could be reached in an extensive manner. However, the continuance of this approach would entail a risk of having an unhealthy financial performance, according to some theoretical and empirical findings. In this context, some MFIs may switch to serve better-off customers resulting in the increase of their respective average sizes of loans.

ii Dependent variable as a composite index (average size of loan plus the percentage of male clients)

It is hypothesized that the granting of small loans as well as the servicing more women clients through the introduction of loan products for women would improve the depth of outreach. This is based in line with the common understanding that women focused credit programs of MFIs are effective in addressing the issues of poverty favorably. The microfinance practitioners assume in general that women are better represented among hard-core poor; and they are willing to make repayment of loans better than their male counterparts. They are also regarded as paying more attention to the social welfare of their children, in particular on health and educational aspects. The composite variable is useful to capture more information in measuring outreach aspects. The value of this variable is converted to the natural logarithm in order to get the advantage of linearity.

iii Explanatory variables

There are several time-variants and a set of dummy variables representing the independent variables. OSS, percentage of women borrowers, number of branch outlets, total expense ratio, logarithm of gross loan balance, cost per borrower, number of female loan officers employed and logarithm of total assets are used as time-varying variables. Individual-based lending and group-based lending are represented by two dummy variables. Two interaction variables are created by multiplying each dummy variable of individual-based lending and group-based lending with the OSS of each MFI for each year of operations that was taken into consideration for this study.

A fixed effects panel data model has been adopted to examine the hypotheses one to seven (1-7).

RESEARCH DESIGN AND METHOD - MODEL II

Model II was developed in relation to the hypothesis whether one could accept or reject the claim that focusing on group lending by an MFI has any negative impact on its OSS. The effectiveness of MFIs in reaching the poor in relation to sustainability is measured by linking the depth dimension of outreach with the financial performance.

Description of Variables

Table 4.2 Variable Description - Model II

Variable Name	Label	Description
Dummy OSS (Dependent)	OSSD	1 if Firm is Financially Self-Sufficient (i.e. OSS>=100 percent) and 0 otherwise
Gross Loan Balance	GLBL	Log of gross loan balance ('000) = ln GLB
Equity	TEQL	Log of value of total equity ('000) = lnTEQ
Debt Equity Ratio	DER	Total debt/Total equity
Outreach	ALBL	Log of average loan balance per borrower = lnALB
Total Expense Ratio	TER	(Financial expense + Operating expense + Write-off amount)/Assets
Experience	XPR	Number of years that the MFI is in operation
Area of Operation	AOP	Number of districts in operation/24
Branch Network	NOO	Number of branches in operation including head office
Female Loan Officers	FLOs	Number of female loan officers
Individual-based Lending	LID	1 if MFI implements individual lending vigorously and 0 otherwise
Group-based Lending	LGD	1 if MFI implements group lending vigorously and 0 otherwise
Active Borrowers	BRR	Number of borrowers who transact with the MFI ('000)

Source: Based on Quayes (2012), Kumar Kar (unpub.) and Cull, Demirguc-Kunt, and Morduch (2007), CGAP (Consultative Group to Assist the Poorest) (2003)

The preliminary estimates show that six variables, gross loan balance, experience, area of operation, branch network, number of female loan officers and individual-based lending are non-significant in the determination of regression results.

Determination of Dependent and Independent Variables

One of the important research questions of this study is to find out whether there is a difference in sustainability according to the types of lending schemes adopted by MFIs. It is assumed that the manner in which the activities and operations of MFIs have been designed and implemented could be decisive in achieving the profit motivation objective or poverty outreach objective of such MFIs. For instance, welfarists argue that the profit motivation of MFIs makes them sustainable, but at the cost of excluding the poor. The possible drift of MFIs from reaching the poor could be curtailed through managerial interventions and adoption of novel schemes of operations, according to empirical evidence.

In this model, the sustainability objectives of MFIs are evaluated in terms of two different microfinance lending schemes they implement, the individual lending method and group lending method. Group formation and inculcating the use of good habits of banking among group members are some of the pre-conditions to be fulfilled for the successful implementation of GLSs, whereas in individual lending, such close supervision by MFIs is not a necessity. In the latter case, the MFIs concerned are supposed to address the problem of proper information unavailability on prospective clients as well.

In view of the foregoing facts, this research has a valid question to raise, i.e., whether any lending approach adopted by an MFI has a significant impact on its financial sustainability. In this context, variables for the model testing have been selected, after leaving insignificant variables out.

In this analysis, a binomial logistic regression is used, where the dependent variable, financial sustainability can have two possible outcomes (i.e., 1 for sustainable years where OSS is greater than or equal to 100 and 0 otherwise). Probability scores are estimated as predicted values of the dependent variable.

The logit regression model is given below (Variables as described under Table 4.2 are applicable).

$$P(OSSD) = \alpha + \beta 1 lnGLB + \beta 2 lnTEQ + \beta 3 DER + \beta 4 lnALB + \beta 5 TER + \beta 6 XPR + \beta 7 AOP + \beta 8 NOO + \beta 9 FLO + \beta 10 LID + \beta 11 LGD + \beta 12 BRR$$

RATIONALE FOR THE SELECTION OF VARIABLES

Average Loan Balance per Borrower

The depth of outreach refers to the level of services available to the poor through any financial institution quantitatively and qualitatively, which can reduce their level of poverty. There is no information to assess the level of poverty or income level of each client in the effort of examining whether the services provided by a particular MFI have impacted on these variables. Therefore, as an alternate proxy in assessing the depth of outreach, the average size of a loan is widely adopted in the literature (Quayes 2012; Hisako 2009; Cull, Demirguc-Kunt, and Morduch 2007; Kumar Kar unpub.; Schreiner 2002). The Microbanking Bulletin, published by the MIX Market, also adopts the average loan size in comparison with GDP Per Capita (PPP) to measure the depth of outreach.

With regard to the average size of a loan, Quayes (2012, 3423-24) indicates that "although it is not a perfect measure of poverty level, it is an excellent proxy for depth of outreach as there is a strong positive correlation between income level and the size of loans." Even though an average size of a loan may have problems of comparison in multi country analysis, it will be a satisfactory and acceptable proxy for depth of outreach for a single country analysis.

It is presumed in our research that an MFI is bound to cater to small-scale borrowers by offering them with smaller loans at affordable prices. Conversely, forgetting this responsibility and drifting away from clients who are poor, an MFI could seek out comparatively better-off clients. The first approach implies a smaller average loan or better outreach while the adoption of second approach would result in increase of the average size of a loan and limiting outreach. Hulme and Mosley (1996) point out that staff members of MFIs may prefer not to include the core poor, since lending to them is seen as extremely risky. This implies that MFIs should keep minimizing risk through the grant of larger size loans to not so poor who are creditworthy to receive such loans.

Percentage of Female Clients

It is assumed, based on empirical evidence that poor women who receive loans from MFIs would directly channel their income of the projects to the betterment of the welfare of their families. The resulting impact of poverty due to MFIs' involvement is captured by the econometric model through the inclusion of proportion of women receiving loans against men as a variable. However, women representation was captured by the composite index through the inclusion of the percentage of male borrowers (not by the percentage of female borrowers), in order to facilitate the statistical interpretation.

According to Hermes and Lensink (2007), it has been established that women are more reliable, have higher repayment ratios and play a very important role in reducing poverty within households. Moreover, Pitt and Khandker (1998) state that women use a substantial part of their income for the health and education of their children. Premarathne, Senanayake and Warnasuriya (2012) show that women empowerment is feasible through the introduction of novel approaches and distribution channels by MFIs, particularly under the formation of SHGs.

Gross Loan Portfolio

The gross loan portfolio is a standard measure of determining the size of an MFI. The volume of loans may increase with the increase of the number of borrowers or/and average sizes of the loans. If the total value of loans increases due to the increase of average sizes of loans, provided that the number of loans remain the same, there is a negative impact on outreach, as both gross loan portfolio and average sizes of loans move towards same direction. However, if there is a negative relationship between these two variables while gross loan portfolio is increasing, it can be concluded that outreach has increased by serving to more and more small-scale borrowers.

Operational Self-Sufficiency (OSS)

In this study, an attempt was made to observe whether the emphasis on financial performance of an MFI has a negative impact on its outreach efforts. Further, we also examine whether different lending schemes adopted by MFIs affect their financial efficiency in a different manner. OSS is defined in the microfinance literature, as total financial revenue as a percentage of the sum of financial expense, operating expense and loan loss provision and the same definition is applied to OSS referred to in this research as well. The financial performance is captured through the use of a dummy variable. Accordingly, financial sustainability takes the value 1 if the OSS is greater than or equal to 100 percent, and 0 if it is less than 100 percent.

Loan Delivery Method

MFIs can adopt various lending methods to reach the poor. Atapattu (2009) has identified that, in Sri Lanka, such lending can occur through various schemes such as village banking, group lending, credit unions co-operatives, SHGs, individual lending and ROSCAS/Seettu. Our research would classify MFIs into two groups of which, one group includes those MFIs that focus on group-based lending, while the other group includes MFIs that focus on individual-based lending.

SUMMARY

In this chapter, the analytical framework is presented by looking into key important areas such as different aspects of outreach of microfinance, the poverty lending approach and financial systems approach, resource requirements to increase income and manifestation of reduction of poverty and cost of outreach to MFIs.

Hypotheses of the study are connected to the examination of the relationship between poverty outreach versus sustainability of the MFIs as well as the relationship between OSS and lending schemes adopted by MFIs. Having studied the mandates of MFIs operating in Sri Lanka, a sample of 50 MFIs was selected for the study.

Microfinance literature is rich with the use of quantitative techniques such as multiple regressions including panel data models, in assessing the relationship between financial sustainability and poverty outreach. Accordingly, a panel data series is used to derive statistical parameters that could shed light on whether financial sustainability and poverty outreach could be achieved simultaneously or whether there is a trade-off between these two variables in the context of MFIs operating in Sri Lanka.

Further, this study adopts a logistic regression to assess the impact of microfinance delivery models on the financial sustainability of MFIs.

CHAPTER 5

DATA ANALYSIS AND RESEARCH FINDINGS

INTRODUCTION

This chapter provides a detailed analysis of data followed by a discussion of the research findings. Data and information were primarily analyzed in order to identify, describe and explore the relationship between financial sustainability and poverty outreach of MFIs. Further, this study also focused on examining the relationship between lending schemes and financial sustainability of MFIs.

As discussed in chapter 1, several research studies have found that a mission drift in microfinance does not occur under certain given situations. Amidst this backdrop, identification of conditions under which MFIs are in a position to concurrently achieve profitability and the depth of outreach is important. There are strong arguments for that the 'win-win' proposition is unattainable particularly when MFIs focus on reaching the absolute poor. Both the outreach objectives and financial performance could be pursued successfully if MFIs adopt effective strategies, particularly in relation to credit delivery, pricing and human resources management.

Empirical evidence has proven that the profitability of a firm, among others is strongly related to a firm's commitment and capability towards innovation and capturing the market. Similarly, the adoption of operational and strategic measures in a dynamic and innovative manner is essential for an MFI to increase its market penetration (depth and breadth of outreach). In this regard, attractive lending products available at affordable cost to the customer play a crucial role. In contrast, an MFI could also follow a different strategy in a manner that would limit its focus on the poorest of the poor in favor of catering to high-end clients, aimed at improving its financial performance. Having analyzed the above contexts, we developed several hypotheses to be tested through appropriate econometric models in order to arrive at certain decisions relating to the research questions of this study. Accordingly, this chapter presents results of the econometric tests carried out, and the interpretation of these results in line with relevant theoretical and empirical findings.

DATASET

Sri Lanka has a microfinance sector comprising a variety of institutions to serve the poor as highlighted in Table 3.9. The mission of each category of MFIs was reviewed in the context of its strategy towards achieving sustainability versus poverty outreach. Accordingly, the MFIs that are pursuing financial performance disregarding poverty outreach or poverty outreach disregarding financial performance, according to their respective mandates, were excluded from the sample.

This analysis is based on a panel dataset compiled from a sample of 50 MFIs that comprised 922 branches by end 2012, including the head office. Accordingly, outreach data and financial data were compiled for each MFI, ranging from a minimum of 2 years and maximum of 6 years during the period of 2007 to 2012, depending on the availability of data. This sample of MFIs is chosen irrespective of the size in terms of the assets, loans and number of clients of each MFI, with the view of minimizing sampling errors.

DESCRIPTIVE AND INFERENTIAL STATISTICS

The sample of this study consists of PSB, SDBL, five Non-Bank Financial Institutions (NBFIs), four Limited Liability Companies, 10 Companies Limited by Guarantee, three Public Liability Companies and 26 NGOs. Details of these MFIs by type of institution, registration and supervision are given in Table 5.1.

Table 5.1 MFIs by Type, Registration and Supervision

Type of Institution	No.	Registration	Supervision
Licensed Specialized Banks (LSBs)	2	Banking Act, No. 30 of 1988 as amended and Monetary Law Act, No. 58 of 1949 (MLA) as amended	Central Bank
Non-Bank Financial Institutions (NBFIs)	5	Finance Business Act, No. 42 of 2011	Central Bank
Companies (Ltd Liability)	4	Companies Act, No. 7 of 2007	self-regulated
Companies (Ltd by Guarantee)	10	Companies Act, No. 7 of 2007	self-regulated
Companies (Public Liability)	3	Companies Act, No. 7 of 2007	self-regulated
NGOs	26	Voluntary Social Service Organizations (Registration and Supervision) Act, No. 31 of 1980 as amended	self-regulated
Total	50		

Source: Central Bank of Sri Lanka
    Microfinance Review - Sri Lanka, Analysis and Performance Report 2012

Table 5.2 provides the details with regard to the size of the sample according to the number of branches, number of clients, volume of loans and deposits.

Table 5.2 MFIs by Branches, Outreach, Loans and Deposits - 2012

Description	Sampled Data (LSBs+NBFIs+Companies+NGOs)	Population (Without TCCSs, *Samurdhi* and CRBs)
Number of Institutions/ Branches	922 254 (RDB) + 80 (SDBL)+ 38 (LFCs)+ 550 (Other MFIs in the Sample)	2894 254 (RDB) + 80 (SDBL) + 60 (LFCs) + 2500[1] (Other MFIs)
	31.86 percent	

Client Outreach	2,083,213	2,438,077
	756,695 (RDB) + 346,816 (SDBL) + 180,321 (LFCs) +799,381(Other MFIs in the Sample)	756,695 (RDB)+ 346,816 (SDBL) + 1,334,566 (Other MFIs)
	85.45 percent (Approximately)	
Loan Portfolio (LKR Mn)	115,921	216,038
	53,750 (RDB) + 17,919 (SDBL)+9702 (LFCs) + 34,550 (Other MFIs in the Sample)	(53,750 (RDB) + 17,919 (SDBL) + n.a. (2500 Other MFIs)
	53.66 percent=115,921/216,038 (Approximately)	
Deposits (LKR Mn)	72,713 54,710 (RDB) + 18,003 (SDBL)+ n.a. (Other MFIs in the Sample)	185,835 54,710 (RDB) + 18,003 (SDBL)+ n.a. (2500 Other MFIs)
	39.1 percent=72,713/185,835 (Approximately)	

Source: Based on Data Collected on MFIs

[1] Assuming that each NGO has only one office.
n.a.: Not available

Classifications of 50 MFIs in the sample by age, size and cost per borrower are given in Tables 5.3, 5.4 and 5.5 respectively.

Table 5.3 shows that 24 percent of MFIs fall within the age category of 15-20 years, while 64 percent of MFIs have been in microfinance operations for more than 10 years. It is also a noteworthy feature that six MFIs or 12 percent of the sampled MFIs have been in microfinance business over 25 years whereas seven MFIs or 14 percent of the sampled MFIs have had less than five years of experience in microfinance.

Table 5.3 A Classification of MFIs by Experience - 2012

Number of Years	Number of MFIs	Number of MFIs as a Percentage
1-05	7	14
5-10	11	22
10-15	5	10
15-20	12	24

20-25	9	18
>25	6	12
Total	**50**	**100**

Source: Based on Data Collected on MFIs

According to Table 5.4, small MFIs within the sample with less than LKR 50 Million loan portfolio each, account for 44 percent of total number of MFIs, while 32 percent of the MFIs have loan portfolio valued more than LKR 200 Million each. As far as asset portfolio is concerned, 46 percent of the MFIs had recorded asset portfolio valued more than LKR 200 Million each, as at end 2012. The number of MFIs with a loan portfolio and asset portfolio more than LKR 1000 Million each stood at 12 percent and 16 percent of the sample respectively.

Table 5.4 A Classification of MFIs by Loan Size and Asset Size - 2012

Size (LKR Mn)	Loans		Assets	
	Number of MFIs	Number of MFIs as a Percentage	Number of MFIs	Number of MFIs as a Percentage
<50	22	44	14	28
50-100	4	8	5	10
100-200	8	16	8	16
200-500	6	12	9	18
500-1000	4	8	6	12
>1000	6	12	8	16
Total	**50**	**100**	**50**	**100**

Source: Based on Data Collected on MFIs

The total annual cost per borrower [(financial cost + operational cost + other costs)/total number of borrowers] varies among 50 MFIs as shown in Table 5.5. For instance, MFIs with less than LKR 2,000/- cost per borrower represented 20 percent of the sampled MFIs while 34 percent of the sampled MFIs had the cost per borrower between LKR 2,000/- to LKR 4,000/- during 2012. There were six MFIs in the sample that recorded more than LKR 10,000/- cost per borrower during the same year.

Table 5.5 A Classification of MFIs by Annual Cost per Borrower - 2012

Cost per Borrower (LKR)	Number of MFIs	Number of MFIs as a Percentage
<2000	10	20
2000-4000	17	34
4000-6000	4	8
6000-8000	9	18
8000-10000	4	8
>10000	6	12
Total	**50**	**100**

Source: Based on Data Collected on MFIs

It is obvious that main expenditure items involving screening customers, follow-up projects and documentation vary widely from one MFI to another, resulting in differences in cost per borrower among the MFIs. The problem of asymmetric information associated with the credit markets that serve people in low-income groups has been identified as the main cause for the high share of total cost of servicing a loan particularly screening customers and monitoring their activities (Beck, Demirguc-Kunt, and Levine 2004). Further, MFIs also face major problems such as low financial literacy of the poor and lack of collateral possessed by them when implementing a pro-poor credit policy. The differences of the cost per borrower show that the MFIs in Sri Lanka are no exception to these generalized situations.

Moreover, the following can be inferred from the information compiled on the loans granted by the MFIs which have been selected for this study:

i.   Loans in most cases are collateral free and typically supported by inter-se-guarantee or dependent on non-traditional collaterals such as past repayments and savings patterns.

ii. Average loan amount per borrower, though small, has increased over the years (e.g., the average size of a loan from an MFI in 2006/07 stood at LKR 84,000/- while this was LKR 103,745/- in 2012 according to relevant data from the sampled MFIs.).

iii. Non-financial services such as training and marketing facilities are extended to borrowers by linking such facilities with the use of funds. There are field officers of many MFIs who are trained to conduct training programs for potential borrowers on the preparation of project proposals, development of entrepreneurship, promotion of savings habits etc.

iv. Loan penetration into remote villages and rural poor is comparatively high. The GTZ-ProMiS Survey 2006/07 showed that 89 percent of the total outlets of MFIs had been established in rural areas while the corresponding figure for the sampled MFIs as at end 2012 was 86 percent.

v.   It is important to note that the loans from MFIs have been obtained for income generating activities as well as other purposes such as consumption and emergencies. It has been observed that there is no real obligatory requirement from the lender to discipline the borrower in respect of the use of borrowed funds.

For instance, the GTZ-ProMiS Survey 2006/07 indicates that only 35 percent of total volume of loans had been utilized for agriculture and businesses/enterprises while the share of consumption, emergencies and settlement of loans stood at as much as 28 percent of total volume of loans. Data from sampled MFIs show that around 35 percent - 43 percent of the value of loans granted by them was for agriculture and related purposes.

TESTING HYPOTHESES - MODEL I

The econometric analysis relating to the relationship between sustainability and the outreach of MFIs in Sri Lanka, consists of several preliminary steps including mainly the checking of the appropriateness of the model before discussing the results. However, this book focusses on the interpretation of the results rather than discussing the preliminary steps.

Summary Statistics - Model I

Summary statistics (values are in USD) relating to Model I is given in Table 5.6. It is evident from the Table 5.6 that there are large standard deviations, reflecting significant variations in data in respect of some variables.

Table 5.6 Summary Statistics - Model I

Label	Variable Name	Mean	Std. Dev.
ALBL	Outreach 1 (log) (Dependent)	-0.24203	0.557888
ALMBL	Outreach 2 (log) (Dependent)	2.320325	1.590964
ASTL	MFI Size (log)	6.783201	2.266155
CPB	Cost per Borrower	47.98132	45.69382
FLOs	Female Loan Officers	24.17578	65.28511
GLBL	Gross Loan Balance (log)	6.460126	2.243111
NOO	Branch Network	17.23346	39.17439
OSS	Operational Self-Sufficiency	139.4608	70.74088
TER1	Total Expense Ratio	37.95244	12.2802
WBR	Women Borrowers (Percentage)	79.21182	18.64541
	Dummy Variables		
OSSD	Dummy OSS	0.603113	0.490207
LID	Individual-based Lending	0.357977	0.480341
LGD	Group-based Lending	0.579767	0.494559

	Interaction Variables		
OSSG	Log of OSS x LGD	1.160596	0.99924
OSSI	Log of OSS x LID	0.729471	0.985234

Source: Based on Data Collected on MFIs

Summary of the Regression Results

The summary results of the two regressions are given in Tables 5.8 and 5.9.

Table 5.7 Summary Results - Regression 1

Variable	Regression 1 (ALBL as Dependent Variable[a])	
	Coefficient	P Value
C	0.979077*	0.0057
OSS	-0.004340*	0.0000
GLBL	-0.357542*	0.0000
WBR	-0.074318*	0.0000
TER	-0.012685*	0.0000
NOO	-0.006463*	0.0000
ASTL	-0.653177*	0.0000
CPB	0.007024*	0.0000
FLOs	0.023139***	0.0848
LGD	0.153371**	0.0148
LID	0.179120**	0.0133
OSSD	-0.067291*	0.0119
OSSG	-1.089903*	0.0007
OSSI	2.229655*	0.0000
R-squared	0.673129	
Adjusted R-squared	0.647817	
F-statistic	12.86917	
Prob(F-statistic)	0.000000	
Durbin-Watson stat	1.430748	

Source: Based on Data Collected on MFIs

*, ** and *** denote significance at the 1 percent, 5 percent and 10 percent levels, respectively.

[a] Log of average loan balance per borrower (ALBL) is the dependent variable for regression 1.

Table 5.8 Summary Results - Regression 2

Variable	Regression 2 (ALMBL as Dependent Variable[a])	
	Coefficient	P Value
C	10.81587*	0.0000
OSS	-0.002695**	0.0454
GLBL	-0.380787**	0.0138
TER	-0.029083*	0.0000
NOO	-0.001480**	0.0104
ASTL	-0.696164*	0.0002
CPB	0.006408*	0.0004
FLOs	-0.002482*	0.0045
LGD	-0.083082**	0.0113
LID	0.060729**	0.0146
OSSD	-0.380184**	0.0114
OSSG	-0.474099**	0.0024
R-squared	0.801600	
Adjusted R-squared	0.780987	
F-statistic	38.88819	
Prob (F-statistic)	0.000000	
Durbin-Watson stat	1.597082	

Source: Based on Data Collected on MFIs

*, ** and *** denote significance at the 1 percent, 5 percent and 10 percent levels, respectively.
[a] Log of composite index of average loan balance per borrower plus the percentage
of male borrowers (ALMBL) is the dependent variable for regression 2.

Interpretation of the Results

Regression 1 with ALBL as the dependent variable produced an adjusted R^2 of 0.65 whereas regression 2 with the composite index ALMBL as the dependent variable produced an adjusted R^2 of 0.78. A satisfactory level of goodness of fit is evidenced by the R^2 value of each regression run.

Results of the regression 1 indicate that OSS has a positive effect on outreach, which is significant at the 01 percent level of significance (a negative coefficient on OSS indicates a positive impact of financial performance on outreach). For instance, an additional one unit increase of OSS is associated with the 0.43 percent decrease of average loan, according to regression 1. Thus, we accept the alternative hypothesis that OSS contributes positively in improving poverty outreach in Sri Lanka.

It can also be inferred that focusing on the poor is not a barrier for any MFI to achieve financial success, given the fact that MFIs adopt correct policies to recover the money that they lend to the customers. The financial success of an MFI, is explicitly linked to outreach efforts which are broadly intertwined with the market share and complemented through cost efficiency among others.

Similarly, according to regression 2, the ALMBL would be reduced by 0.26 percent for each one unit increase in OSS. Hence, we accept the alternative hypothesis that there is a positive relationship between financial sustainability and depth of outreach measured in terms of average loan balance per borrower plus the percentage of male borrowers. This can be further viewed as a fact that MFIs are in a position to increase outreach by catering to more women clients without creating any adverse impact on sustainability.

The third alternative hypothesis tests whether the effect of group loans on the poverty outreach is positive. The output from regression 1 can be interpreted as, the MFIs with high emphasis on group lending are estimated to have a 15 percent smaller average loan balance per borrower than MFIs that do not have GLSs as their key approach to lending. Similarly, the output from regression 2 can be interpreted as, the MFIs with high emphasis on group lending are estimated to have a 8.3 percent smaller AMLBL (meaning smaller average loan balance and increased share of women borrowers) than MFIs that do not have GLSs as their key approach to lending. The regression results further confirm that when group lending becomes a useful mechanism for MFIs to address poverty effectively, individual lending affects negatively on poverty outreach. As highlighted in the literature review chapter, the GLSs can be adopted to avoid or mitigate the problems of adverse selection and moral hazard prevailing in rural credit markets and this view is empirically tested to be accurate according to the regression results.

A dummy variable has been included in the respective regressions, to represent those MFIs which are self-sufficient financially, in order to examine whether operationally self-sufficient MFIs can make a positive impact on achieving poverty outreach (hypothesis 4). According to regressions 1 and 2, financially self-sufficient MFIs are estimated to have a 6.7 percent smaller ALBL per borrower at the 1 percent level of significance or 38 percent smaller ALMBL at the 5 percent level of significance, than the MFIs which are not financially self-sufficient. These results further confirm that, after attaining financial self-sufficiency, MFIs have the capacity to improve outreach in a significant way.

The alternative hypothesis 5 states that, if the size of the assets of an MFI increases, then there will be an increase in poverty outreach as well. The respective coefficient values of regression 1 and regression 2 confirm that, the increase of total assets by 1 percent is associated with the reduction of ALBL by 0.65 percent and ALMBL by 0.70 percent, both of which are measured at the 5 percent level of significance. The MFIs which have larger volume of assets are generally placed at a better leverage to change their strategic direction, as reflected through the relationship of assets to outreach of an MFI.

Employment of female loan officers (FLOs) has been more effective in reaching poor according to regression analysis output. It is observed that the employment of males for the same job has been less effective. ALBL would be reduced by 2.3 percent at the 10 percent level of significance while ALMBL would be reduced by 0.25 percent at the 1 percent level of significance for the employment of one additional female loan officer by an MFI, according to the respective regressions results. This may be because of the fact that the FLOs have strong capacity and capability to develop close interaction with female clients who are in poverty groups.

Hypothesis 7, of which alternative hypothesis assumes that if an MFI establishes more branch offices (NOO), then there will be an increase in poverty outreach. This relates to the point of view that the establishment of more branches would strengthen the ability of an MFI to closely interact with the poor who have been hitherto denied banking facilities. According to regression 1, the establishment of an additional branch office would result in 0.65 percent decrease in the average size of a loan at the 1 percent level of significance. Similarly, regression 2 output shows that establishment of branches additionally, will result in decrease of ALMBL by 0.15 percent at the 01 percent level of significance. This means that, in addition to reducing the average size of a loan, branch establishment would also help to cater to more women clients. Overall, the results confirm that the benefits of having more branch offices in terms of reaching the poor outweigh the cost of establishment and operations of such branches.

It is also worthwhile to interpret other coefficient values of regressions 1 and 2 in order to justify validity of certain other results already discussed. For instance, the total expense of an MFI compared with its assets (TER) is positively correlated with outreach, implying the fact that the increase of cost in relation to assets of an MFI would help in promoting smaller loans. Accordingly, one unit increase in TER would reduce the ALBL by 1.3 percent or ALMBL by 2.9 percent at the 1 percent level of significance.

It is also evident from the results of each regression that the increase of women borrowers substantially contributes towards achieving poverty outreach. According to the first regression, the average size of a loan would be decreased by 7.4 percent at the 1 percent level of significance due to increase of female clients by 1 percent. This is an obvious indication that MFIs could achieve depth of outreach if they pursue a policy of extending more loan facilities to the female clients instead of male clients.

The cost per borrower (CPB) is negatively correlated with the outreach objectives of MFIs. The relevant coefficients show that the one unit increase of CPB would result in increase of ALBL and ALMBL by 0.70 percent and 0.64 percent, respectively, at the 1 percent level of significance, implying the fact that cost efficiency is an essential factor in improving outreach. This further reflects the fact that loan schemes commonly adopted by MFIs do not necessarily facilitate them to reduce costs. Therefore, MFIs are required to adopt novel methods such as group lending to reduce cost per borrower and achieve depth of outreach in a satisfactory manner.

The interaction variable constructed by multiplying self-sufficiency with the group lending dummy variable (OSSG), reports a negative coefficient in respect of each regression indicating that it affects outreach in a positive manner. However, the interaction variable constructed by multiplying self-sufficiency with the individual lending dummy variable (OSSI) shows that it contributes negatively in promoting outreach.

TESTING HYPOTHESES - MODEL II

The research question whether the sustainability of MFIs is differently affected by types of lending schemes adopted by them needs to be addressed through the application of a different econometric methodology.

A close examination of the operations of MFIs selected for this study suggests that most MFIs pursue sustainability while paying attention to improve poverty outreach. It has been observed from data analysis of this study that outreach is feasible alongside sustainability. However, according to the theoretical viewpoint of Welfarists, the profit earnings of firms take place only at the cost of exclusion of the poor. In this context, we assume that MFIs are left with the option of adopting novel schemes that could reduce their operational cost and improve effectiveness in reaching the poor. The willingness to embark on innovative programs would be manifested in key operations of MFIs, in particular with regard to their lending operations. Innovative lending schemes would be useful in offsetting any negative impact likely to come from other variables affecting financial sustainability.

In view of the necessity to conduct statistical tests, the MFIs in the sample of this study have been classified in terms of the main microfinance lending schemes they implement, i.e., individual lending schemes and GLSs. In general, the effective adoption of the GLSs is dependent on the degree of close guidance of group members and the relationship being built with them by staff of financial institutions to deal with problems of information asymmetry.

In the above context, a valid hypothesis was established to examine whether any outreach efforts by MFIs such as the use of innovative lending schemes, affect financial sustainability of such MFIs favorably. In this connection, a Logit model can be employed to estimate the impact of factors on financial sustainability of MFIs including the adoption of GLSs and individual lending schemes.

Summary Statistics

Table 5.9 Summary Statistics - Model II

Label	Variable Name	Mean	Std. Dev.
OSSD	Dummy OSS	0.603113	0.490207
TEQL	Equity (log)	5.218842	2.333728
DER	Debt Equity Ratio	10.09152	24.95177
ALBL	Outreach	-0.24203	0.55788
TER	Total Expense Ratio	37.95244	12.2802
LGD	Group-based Lending	0.579767	0.494559
BRR	Active Borrowers ('000)	37.18	118.7

Source: Based on Data Collected on MFIs

Table 5.10 Summary Results - Regression 3

Variable	Regression 3 (P(OSSD)) as Dependent Variable	
	Coefficient	P Value
TEQL	0.353644	0.0000
DER	-0.017039	0.0076
TER	-0.097192	0.0000
ALBL	-0.441725	0.0869

LGD	0.371106	0.0084
BRR	0.042323	0.0662
Mean dependent variance		0.605469
S.E. of regression		0.425436
Sum squared residuals		45.24886
Log likelihood		-133.1786
Deviance		266.3571
Avg. log likelihood		-0.520229
Observations with Dependent Variable=0 [a]		101
Observations with Dependent Variable=1 [a]		155

Source: Based on Data Collected on MFIs

[a] 1 for sustainable years where OSS is greater than or equal to 100 and 0 otherwise.

Based on the above results, logit regression with statistically significant coefficients is shown below:

$$P(OSSD) = \alpha + 0.3536TEQL - 0.0170DER - 0.0972TER - 0.44173ALBL + 0.3711LGD + 0.0423BR$$

According to the results of logit regression, the variables such as Equity (TEQL), Debt Equity Ratio (DER), Total Expense Ratio (TER), Average Loan Balance per Borrower (ALBL), Group-Based Lending (LGD) and Number of Borrowers (BRR) are statistically significant. The coefficient values of logit regression are interpreted differently in comparison with those of a normal multiple regression. For instance, according to Table 5.12, a 1 percent increase in TEQL will change the z-score of Pr (Y=1) by 0.353644 which is significant at the 5 percent level.

Interpretation of Results

Coefficients of regression 3 can be interpreted using marginal effects derived for a one unit change in each variable on the probability of getting OSS. Marginal effects calculated using E-views 8 are given in Table 5.14.

Table 5.11 Marginal Effect of Variables (Probability of OSS > 100 percent)

TEQL	0.118351
DER	-0.005702
TER	-0.032526
ALBL	-0.147828
LGD	0.124195
BRR	0.007677

Source: Based on Data Collected on MFIs

However, the probability of getting OSS is very small in respect of each case as revealed by Table 5.14. This is because, the mean value of each variable where the estimated probability of getting OSS is already high and therefore the increase in any variable can have only a very marginal difference.

The alternative hypothesis 8 states that if an MFI adopts GLSs more than the individual loan schemes, then this action will result in a positive relationship of GLSs with the sustainability of the said MFI. This is because group loans are considered conducive for achieving poverty outreach better than individual loans. The logit regression provides us with a clear indication that the MFIs which operate GLSs have the probability of achieving OSS 12.4 percent higher than those MFIs that do not use group lending as their main method of lending.

Certain theories on microfinance have highlighted problems of credit accessibility and unavailability of comprehensive details on prospective clients. These theories are well focused on information frictions and ensuing failures of credit markets that bring about inefficiency (Luoto, Mcintosh, and Wydick 2007). The MFIs which operate at grass root levels are capable of designing strategies to address the problems of adverse selection and moral hazard prevailing in credit markets. For instance, GLSs introduced by MFIs are useful in managing transaction related risks by sharing the same with the entire community where the poor live. Low risk associated with high recovery rates ensures better financial performance as reflected by the regression results.

The regression output also shows that the increase of equity of MFIs positively contribute to achieve OSS. Accordingly, a 1 percent increase in equity increases the probability of attaining financial sustainability by 11.8 percent. Equity represents the owners' fund that would augment self-reliance of the MFIs. MFIs with less dependence on borrowed funds would be able to extend small loans while maintaining cost efficiency.

Another important conclusion that can be derived from the results of regression 3 is that the one unit increase in depth of outreach (one unit decrease in average loan size) increases the probability of reaching OSS by 14.8 percent. This could happen due to the new loans being extended to the poor benefit the MFIs mainly because of the high recovery rates and efficient cost management.

The DER shows a negative relationship with the financial performance of an MFI. For instance, the one unit increase in DER decreases the probability of attaining financial sustainability by 0.5 percent. The behavior of the DER is in line with our expectation, that when MFIs are required to borrow funds at certain rates of interest and lend such funds extensively, most probably those MFIs cannot generate profits to sustain the business. Hence, the MFIs need to apply a fine balance between borrowed funds and equity funds in order to achieve sustainability.

Marginal effect of TER reported in Table 5.14 indicates that the one unit increase of TER would cause a decrease in the probability of attaining financial sustainability by 3.3 percent. Expenses in relation to asset creation need to be managed for better performance in terms of sustainability, but the statistical analysis proves that MFIs have to make further efforts in achieving cost efficiency.

The increase of active borrowers positively contributes to attain the self-sufficiency of MFIs although the level of such impact is very marginal (For instance, the increase of one batch of active borrowers as defined in the regression would cause an increase in the probability of attaining financial sustainability by 0.8 percent). There is a necessity for the MFIs to reschedule loans and provide other necessary relief to customers or apply stringent measures as provided for by the existing law in order to arrest the likelihood of default of loans. As described under the theoretical concept of strategic default, some borrowers provide inaccurate information to the banks about the income of their projects in order not to repay the loans. The absence of quality information about the borrowers' use of funds on the projects for which the loans have been obtained by them, significantly affect the status of defaults. If the MFIs could obtain correct information about their clients with some appropriate mechanisms in place, the MFIs could realize better financial performance, as confirmed by the regression results.

SUMMARY

In this chapter, having obtained outputs for two regressions under Model I and one regression under Model II using the E-views 8 software, I discussed findings on eight hypotheses applicable to the research.

Results show that the OSS of an MFI is positively related to poverty outreach which is measured in terms of the average loan size per borrower or average loan size per borrower plus percentage of male borrowers. Hence, as far as the MFIs in Sri Lanka are concerned, it can be concluded that there is no inverse relationship between financial performance and the depth of outreach. It is also observed that the MFIs which have more portfolio on group lending perform better in outreach than the MFIs which focus on individual lending. The relationships of many other important variables with poverty outreach variable were also discussed in this chapter.

The assumption, whether the financial performance of MFIs differs by the use of different lending schemes, was tested by the application of Model II. It was found that GLSs, in comparison with the individual loan schemes are very effective in increasing the probability of attaining OSS of an MFI. Model II also explores the relationships of several other variables with the sustainability of an MFI.

CHAPTER 6

CONCLUSIONS, POLICY RELEVANCE AND FURTHER STUDIES

In this concluding chapter, most of the important research findings are further highlighted, particularly in the context of providing insight and policy directions with regard to microfinance in Sri Lanka. Moreover, potential areas for future research that have been identified as important in the course of this study are also mentioned in the interest of exploring a way forward to address broader issues of microfinance in Sri Lanka.

SUMMARY RESULTS

As discussed earlier, there is a hefty debate on the effectiveness of the role of MFIs on poverty reduction. The proponents of the poverty lending approach indicate that if MFIs focus on achieving financial sustainability, they are compelled to depend strictly on market criteria for lending, disregarding the fact that microfinance is meant to be extended to low-income groups at an affordable cost. Consequently, the poor who cannot afford to meet the cost of borrowing and other requirements of lenders, would stay away from credit markets. Even if the MFIs choose to relax certain conditions on lending, it is less likely that such lending would flow to the poorest of the poor. However, on the other hand, the proponents of the financial systems approach stress that empirical evidence does not support the fact that the poor are unable to meet market criteria in applying for the services offered by financial institutions.

The findings of this research would be useful in observing the applicability of competing views expressed by the two schools of thought, and more specifically, the relevance of one of the most widely debated issues of microfinance, the 'mission drift' among researchers, practitioners and policy makers in microfinance, in the context of the operations of MFIs in Sri Lanka.

Chapter 2 is a representation of theory and literature on microfinance relating to main theme of this research. The theories of microfinance, evolved from the broader area of 'rural finance' have been adequately discussed in this chapter. It is observed that subsidized rural credit programs to provide finance to the poor and other disadvantaged groups of societies in many developing countries have been initiated in the past, particularly after 1960s. The supply leading finance theory describes in detail, the theoretical underpinnings of such credit delivery mechanisms. Financial markets in certain developing countries perform lackadaisically, and in the presence of market failures due to problems of adverse selection and moral hazard, interventionist credit delivery mechanisms are justified for the efficient allocation of credit. Further, the role played by the money lenders in the informal sector in developing countries is justified and the existence of dual markets in the rural credit sector is considered to be in order as the lenders and borrowers accomplish some mutual interests. In addition, the savings are recognized as a way of relief to avoid any possible strategic defaults, and meet future exigencies of life and collateral requirements of the lenders. Finally, it is envisaged that in the light of theoretical explanations relating to areas such as income generation, employment creation, recourse to local money lenders, gender empowerment, and social solidarity, there is a vacuum in credit markets that can most probably be filled by microfinance.

Chapter 2 of this study also discusses the literature on microfinance, focusing on the features of microfinance and highlighting other areas of importance that are related to financial sustainability and poverty outreach in microfinance. Accordingly, the literature was reviewed in relation to the grant of small size loans, targeting poor people who lack collaterals as well as opportunities, involvement of more women clients, working in unbanked and remote places by employees and spending relatively high costs on the follow-up activities of projects and documentation among other things. Literature is abundant in support of the view that, focusing more on financial and institutional performance would derail MFIs from targeting social objectives. On the other hand, the overemphasis on the absolute poor would result in overall inefficiency and in this regard, the innovative mechanisms on risk sharing adopted by MFIs, relating to provision of credit, such as group lending, are essentially and appropriately discussed. Despite a vast amount of literature available on microfinance, it was observed that the studies relevant to operations of microfinance in Sri Lanka are available on a very limited scale. Moreover, there is no any macro level study available on the issue of sustainability versus outreach relating to operations of MFIs in Sri Lanka. The present research, therefore is an attempt to fill the said research gap.

MFIs are a special type of credit facilitator for the poor. The current research involving the operations of MFIs in Sri Lanka warranted a detailed analysis to be preceded on the financial sector developments, evolution of macroeconomic conditions including poverty aspects in Sri Lanka. The financial sector development evolves in tandem with the emergence of financial institutions, instruments and markets. Although, a vast body of empirical research has found that there is a positive correlation between economic growth and financial sector development, only a very few studies have explored the relationship between the operations of MFIs and financial development.

The poverty trends of Sri Lanka over a period of few decades and the magnitude of MFIs' operations in reaching the poor in the past, within the broader framework of the financial system, have been appropriately discussed in chapter 3. There has been weak financial intermediation by commercial banks and strong government intervention in the financial sector during the pre-reform period. This trend has, however, reversed with the liberalization of the financial sector, resulting in the establishment of a significant number of foreign and local banks during the post-reform period. Furthermore, there has been an expansion of financial sector infrastructure in the country in response to mainly the growing business of banking, finance and insurance under the liberalization regime.

Theoretically, financial sector growth should cause poverty reduction up to a threshold level of economic development through the growth enhancing effect, but such a relationship would not continue to exist as income inequality, resulting from growth, becomes an impediment. This phenomenon was identified during the post-reform era of the country. It has also been observed that significant changes in poverty levels of Sri Lanka had occurred along with the implementation of some large-scale poverty alleviation schemes. At the same time, there has been an increase in the presence of MFIs in the Sri Lankan financial sector and one could, therefore, rationally deduce that the services offered by these institutions would also have contributed to the reduction of poverty in Sri Lanka.

The analytical framework that has been applied to test the hypotheses of the study is briefly discussed in chapter 4. Accordingly, a panel data model and a logit model were employed to derive statistical parameters useful for arriving at definitive answers to the research questions.

In this study, eight hypotheses were tested with the use of data collected from 50 MFIs in Sri Lanka. Three separate regression analyses were conducted in this regard using the E-views 8 software. Accordingly, the main findings that are derived from the study in relation to microfinance operations in Sri Lanka are summarized as follows:

a) Sustainability, measured in terms of OSS, shows a positive relationship with the depth of poverty outreach, measured in terms of average loan size or a composite index representing average loan size and percentage of male borrowers. The results indicate the applicability and relevancy, to some extent, of the views of welfarists and institutionalists on the poverty lending approach and the financial systems approach. Thus, it is evident that servicing to the poor by MFIs has not caused any adverse impact on MFIs' financial performance.

b) Group-based lending, as against individual-based lending, shows a positive relationship with depth of poverty outreach, confirming the fact that GLSs are effective in managing the problem of information asymmetry prevailing in rural credit markets.

c) Operationally self-sufficient MFIs are capable of achieving poverty outreach successfully, while the MFIs that are not operationally self-sufficient have not shown significant impact in reaching the poor.

d) The size of the asset portfolio of an MFI affects poverty outreach positively. This relationship will persists if the MFIs have the ability to utilize their assets/funds productively and maintain higher rates of recovery on their loans.

e) Employment of female loan officers by MFIs is positively correlated with poverty outreach. This could be partially attributable to the fact that female officers are able to closely interact with female clients in relation to use of funds for the projects.

f) Having more branches by MFIs, particularly in outstation areas, contributes to cater to more clients who are poor. Accordingly, it can be inferred that the benefits of providing services to the clients with the opening of new branches outweigh the cost of operations of such branches.

g) The MFIs which emphasize on and expand group-based lending have the higher probability of achieving sustainability than the MFIs that do not rely on GLSs. The implementation of GLSs are advantageous in identifying prospective customers who could maintain durable and strong relationships with MFIs.

h) Equity funds positively contribute to improve the sustainability of MFIs. This further implies that microfinance cannot be sustained with the excessive reliance on debt financing.

POLICY RELEVANCE

The findings of the research shed light on a few lessons in the Sri Lankan context of microfinance that would be useful to policy makers as well as microfinance practitioners. Implementing a policy that would provide conducive environment for MFIs in Sri Lanka to achieve better financial performance is necessary, as the expansion of their activities to reach the poor is associated with financial sustainability. Further, in the absence of an inverse relationship between the depth of outreach and financial performance of microfinance operations in Sri Lanka, the pursuit of solely the welfarists' demand for MFIs to adopt a poverty-targeted lending or institutionalists' advice for MFIs to focus on sustainability is not warranted. Instead, it is necessary for MFIs to design and adopt policies to achieve an equilibrium in which both the sustainability and poverty outreach objectives can be met. This kind of a policy will facilitate MFIs to manage risks and avoid possible strategic deviation known as mission drift.

Overall, the analysis of the current debates of microfinance in the context of operations of MFIs in Sri Lanka has helped in identifying benchmark role and operations of MFIs for the benefit of the poor in the country. Accordingly, the pragmatic viewpoint acceptable to policy makers as well as regulators is that MFIs should strive to achieve institutional self-sufficiency through the outreach efforts that are beneficial to the people who are in poverty.

Among the significant challenges that are faced by MFIs in Sri Lanka at present, setting a strategy that would strike a balance between the financial goals and social obligations has become a priority. In this regard, it is observed that MFIs need to take complementary actions such as implementation of GLSs to accomplice these twin goals. Overall, there is ample evidence to show that MFIs have been innovative in order to meet the challenges faced by them, particularly through the introduction of new products involving loans and deposits. GLSs are performed by many MFIs in Sri Lanka and such schemes have gathered momentum in bringing about overall cost efficiency and financial sustainability for MFIs. On this basis, it is useful to explore the ways and means available to promote GLSs, particularly with the intention of inculcating, inter alia, good habits of banking and effective utilization of loans by the potential borrowers.

The central theme transpired through this study should not be interpreted by those who are concerned including policy makers to facilitate MFIs in operation of the country to earn exorbitant profits in order to serve the poor effectively. Increasing indebtedness among rural poor in the country has become a cause for concern by relevant authorities in the recent past, and often the actions of unregulated MFIs to charge high interest rates from the borrowers have been cited as the main reason for defaults of loans and consequent increase of indebtedness. Certainly, there are MFIs which compete with each other through subtle ways which have finally paved the way for uninformed clients to secure loans from as many MFIs as possible without having capacity to repay such loans. Further, at present there is no necessity for MFIs to check the status on indebtedness of customers before granting new loan facilities to them, as most of these MFIs are not subject to supervision. In this context, it necessary to implement a proper regulatory system to control the behavior of certain MFIs which compete for earning exorbitant profits through improper actions.

Even though, the MFIs' role in reaching the poor is dependent on the financial success of the MFIs, more stringent measures need to be adopted to ensure that rural poor are not subject to exploitation due to malicious actions by certain MFIs. Especially, the regulators should be able to play a vital role in protecting the borrowers' right to access financial facilities from MFIs under equal and equitable basis. The CBSL has imposed an upper ceiling of 35 percent annual effective interest rate, inclusive of all other charges on micro loans with effect from December 03, 2018. However, this direction applies only to SLCs, whereas the problem of charging unreasonable interest rates from micro level borrowers has been created by various types of NGO MFIs, that are not subject to supervision by the CBSL.

Financial customer protection framework, issued by the CBSL on January 16, 2018 to LFCs, requires these companies to provide complete, clear, concise, accurate and not misleading information about any financial product that will be introduced to customers. This charter also stipulates the LFCs to improve customer awareness, equitable and fair treatment towards customers and complaint handling procedure among others in order to ensure that characteristics of the lending instruments are not misleading. Although these directions would help the borrowers to make informed decisions, the directions are not specifically aimed at providing relief to current micro-loan issues encountered by rural poor including massive indebtedness faced by them. Government policy of providing a relief package to overcome indebtedness issue of micro level borrowers may not be a prudent approach as such policy will be detrimental in the creation of sustainable MFIs as well as clients who could be able to graduate themselves from low income earners to high income earners.

There is a proposal to introduce an Act to regulate and supervise persons engaged in the business of moneylending and the business of microfinance in the near future. This Act might be able to facilitate the introduction of policies for proper market conduct and implement the same in coordination with other stakeholders, particularly in the areas of credit counseling, conduct of awareness programs and gathering information for analytical decision making. Sri Lanka has not applied regulatory provisions that are in existent in other relevant legislations to control unscrupulous money lenders and in this context, the proposed Act would be able to fix this lacuna while expanding the coverage of provision and level of authority to handle many issues of micro lending. However, this job to be spearheaded effectively needs a strong capacity base in terms of manpower and other resources to any authority, as the microfinance sector in Sri Lanka consists of a large number of micro level clients who are poor, the MFI outlets exceeding more than 14000 and also unknown number of money lenders. On the other hand, introduction of any rules and regulations to restrict the current level of operations of MFIs as well as any policies to replace informal sector institutions with more formal sector institutions without conducting any empirical research to understand the real issues of microfinance would be counterproductive.

The MFIs have also given emphasis on the selection of appropriate target groups, substitution of collateral requirement with joint liability schemes, reengineering of internal operations and capacity building of the staff, for the purpose of realizing financial success while reaching the poor successfully. However, it has been observed that the problem of information asymmetry has become a challenge for MFIs under individual-based lending. It is therefore, necessary that MFIs adopt innovative cost reduction methods on a continuous basis in order to achieve sustainability.

Moreover, the achievement of the main goal of financial sustainability and poverty outreach simultaneously require thorough understanding, inter alia, on factors such as scale of individual-based lending, level of branch expansion, selection and recruitment of number of female loan officers and amount of equity capital used. It is also critical in understanding how the assets can be employed efficiently while extending credit in an appropriate manner to more female clients in the light of the findings of this research.

Results of the econometric tests need not be conceived as a complete guidance to prescribe policy recommendations as this study was carried out to achieve certain specific objectives discussed earlier. Certainly, there is no need to scale-up operations in an arbitrary manner, but it is essential to determine the target groups of people to whom the services will be extended in order for MFIs in Sri Lanka to accomplish the task of achieving depth of outreach and sustainability.

DIRECTION FOR FURTHER RESEARCH

In this book, we have presented a data analysis of 50 MFIs which represented 85 percent of client outreach, 54 percent of lending portfolio and 39 percent of deposit portfolio of the MFIs in the country as at end 2012. The study took into consideration the proxies such as the average loan size and number of female clients receiving loans in measuring the depth of outreach. Further, sustainability was assessed in terms of the ability of an MFI to cover its cost (financial cost + operational cost + provision on loan impairment) in relation to its income. Overall, as the findings of the research emanated from the results of two panel data regressions and a Logit regression are sound, there is hardly any need to conduct another research now involving MFIs in Sri Lanka using similar criteria and tools for the same objectives.

However, the depth of poverty outreach and sustainability are broader concepts that may be sometimes viewed and measured differently depending on the context of their use. For instance, the depth of poverty outreach can be considered as the real change of absolute poverty status of a subject whereas sustainability can be viewed as the continuation of the business while attaining certain set of financial targets. Effecting such changes to conceptual and empirical meaning of the variables selected for this study could lead to different outcomes, even if the objectives of the study remain the same.

Further, there are other areas of research which need to be explored in relation to financial sustainability and different other dimensions of microfinance, such as the breadth of outreach, the length of outreach and the scope of outreach of MFIs in Sri Lanka. Conducting research on new areas as suggested, would be beneficial in many ways, in particular in understanding policy insight for overall improvement of microfinance operations of the country.

BIBLIOGRAPHY

Ahmed, S.M., and M.I. Ansari. 1998. "Financial Sector Development and Economic Growth: The South-Asian Experience." *Journal of Asian Economics* 9 (3): 503–17.

Alailima, P.J. 1986, "Social Development Alternatives in Sri Lanka." *Regional Development Dialogue,* 7(1): 103 –132.

Amarathunga, H. 2012. "Finance - Growth Nexus: Evidence from Sri Lanka." *Staff Studies* 40 (1-2): 1–36.

Anand, Sudhir, and S. M. Ravi. Kanbur. 1991. "Public Policy and Basic Needs Provision: Intervention and Achievement in Sri Lanka." In *The Political Economy of Hunger, Vol. 3,* edited by Jean Dreze and Amartya Sen, 59-92. Oxford: Clarendon Press.

Armendáriz, Beatriz. 1999. "On the Design of a Credit Agreement with Peer Monitoring." *Journal of Development Economics* 60 (1): 79–104.

Armendariz, Beatriz, and Ariane Szafarz. 2009. "On Mission Drift in Microfinance Institutions.".In *The Handbook of Microfinance,* edited by Armendariz, Beatriz, and Marc Labie, 341-366.Cambridge: World Scientific Publishing Co. Pte. Ltd.

Armendariz, Beatriz, and Jonathan Morduch. 2011. *The Economics of Microfinance.* New Delhi: PHI Learning Press.

Arun, Thankom. 2005. "Regulating for Development: The Case of Microfinance." *The Quarterly Review of Economics and Finance* 45 (2-3): 346–57.

Asian Development Bank. 2000. "Towards an ADB Microfinance Development Strategy." Accessed December 2, 2014. http://www.adb.org/.../finance-poor-microfinance-development-strategy.

———. 2009. "Grant Assistance to Viet Nam for Formalizing Microfinance Institutions." Accessed December 2, 2014. http://www.adb.org/sites/default/files/project.../42492-012-vie-dpg-13.pdf.

Assefa, Esubalew, Niels Hermes, and Aljar Meesters. 2013. "Competition and the Performance of Microfinance Institutions." *Applied Financial Economics* 23 (9): 767–82.

Atapattu, Anura. 2009. "State of Microfinance in Sri Lanka." Rep. *State of Microfinance in Sri Lanka*. Colombo: Institute of Microfinance (InM).

Athukorala, Premachandra, and Kunal Sen. 2002. *Saving, Investment, and Growth in India*. Delhi: Oxford University Press.

Aubert, Cécile, Alain De Janvry, and Elisabeth Sadoulet. 2009. "Designing Credit Agent Incentives to Prevent Mission Drift in pro-Poor Microfinance Institutions." *Journal of Development Economics* 90 (1): 153–62.

Bagehot, Walter. 1873. *Lombard Street: a Description of the Money Market.: 4th Ed*. London. http://socserv.mcmaster.ca/~econ/ugcm/3ll3/bagehot/lombard.html

Baltagi, Badi H. 2009. *Econometric Analysis of Panel Data. Econometric Analysis of Panel Data*. Chichester: John Wiley & Sons Inc.

Barslund, Mikkel, and Finn Tarp. 2008. "Formal and Informal Rural Credit in Four Provinces of Vietnam." *The Journal of Development Studies* 44 (4): 485–503.

Bateman, Milford. 2010. *Why Doesn't Microfinance Work? The Destructive Rise of Local Neoliberalism.* London: Zed.

Beck, Thorsten, Asli Demirguc-Kunt, and Ross Levine. 2004. "Finance, Inequality, and Poverty: Cross-Country Evidence." *Policy Research Working Paper 3338.* Washington D.C.: World Bank. https://doi:10.3386/w10979.

Berardi, Marco. 2007. "Credit Rationing in Markets With Imperfect Information." *SSRN Electronic Journal.* https://doi.org/10.2139/ssrn.1010965.

Besley, Timothy, and Stephen Coate. 1995. "Group Lending, Repayment Incentives and Social Collateral." *Journal of Development Economics* 46 (1): 1–18.

Bhole, Bharat, and Sean Ogden. 2010. "Group Lending and Individual Lending with Strategic Default." *Journal of Development Economics* 91 (2): 348–63.

Bose, Pinaki. 1998. "Formal–Informal Sector Interaction in Rural Credit Markets." *Journal of Development Economics* 56 (2): 265–80.

Brau, James C., and Gary M Woller. 2004. "Microfinance: A comprehensive Review of the Existing Literature." *Journal of Entrepreneurial Finance and Business Ventures* 9 (1): 1-28.

Braverman, Avishay, and J.luis Guasch. 1986. "Rural Credit Markets and Institutions in Developing Countries: Lessons for Policy Analysis from Practice and Modern Theory." *World Development* 14 (10-11): 1253–67.

Breierova, Lucia, and Esther Duflo. 2004. "The Impact of Education on Fertility and Child Mortality: Do Fathers Really Matter Less Than Mothers?" doi:10.3386/w10513.

Calderón, César, and Lin Liu. 2003. "The Direction of Causality between Financial Development and Economic Growth." *Journal of Development Economics* 72 (1): 321–34.

Cason, Timothy N., Lata Gangadharan, and Pushkar Maitra. 2012. "Moral Hazard and Peer Monitoring in a Laboratory Microfinance Experiment." *Journal of Economic Behavior & Organization* 82 (1): 192–209.

Central Bank of Sri Lanka. 1998. *Economic Progress of Independent Sri Lanka: Published on the Occasion of the Fiftieth Anniversary of the Independence of Sri Lanka.* Colombo: Central Bank of Sri Lanka.

Central Bank of Sri Lanka. 2016. *Economic and Social Statistics of Sri Lanka.* Colombo: Central Bank of Sri Lanka.

Central Bank of Sri Lanka. 2018. *Annual Report.* Colombo: Central Bank of Sri Lanka.

CGAP (Consultative Group to Assist the Poorest). 2003. *Microfinance Consensus Guidelines - Definitions of Selected Financial Terms, Ratios, and Adjustments for Microfinance.* Washington D.C.: World Bank.

Chandrasiri, Sunil. 2008. "Industrial development and poverty reduction experience in Sri Lanka.". In *Development Perspectives-Growth and Equity in Sri Lanka*, Edited by Senanayake Piyadasa,

Wimalaratana, Wijitapure, and De Silva, Amala, 43-68. Colombo: University of Colombo.

Charitonenko, Stephanie, and Dulan de. Silva. 2002. *Commercialization of Microfinance: Sri Lanka*. Manila: Asian Development Bank.

Charitonenko, Stephanie, Anita Campion, and A. Nimal. Fernando. 2004. *Commercialization of Microfinance: Perspectives from South and Southeast Asia*. Manila: Asian Development Bank.

Chaves, Rodrigo A., and Claudio Gonzalez-Vega. 1992. "Principles of Regulation and Prudential Supervision: Should They be Different for Microenterprise Finance Organizations?", *Occasional Paper*, no. 1979. Columbus: The Ohio State University.

Chibba, Michael. 2009. "Financial Inclusion, Poverty Reduction and the Millennium Development Goals." *The European Journal of Development Research* 21 (2): 213–30. https://doi.org/10.1057/ejdr.2008.17.

Christen, Robert Peck. 1997. "Issues in the Regulation and Supervision of Microfinance." In From Margin to Mainstream: The Regulation and Supervision of Microfinance, edited by Rock and Otero. Monograph 11. Somerville, Mass.: ACCION International.

———. 2000. "Commercialization and Mission Drift: The Transformation of Microfinance in Latin America." *CGAP Occasional Paper*, no. 5. *Commercialization and Mission Drift: The Transformation of Microfinance in Latin America*. Washington, D.C.: World Bank.

Christen, Robert Peck, Elisabeth Rhyne, Robert Vogel, and Cressida McKean. 1995. "Maximizing the Outreach of Microenterprise

Finance: An Analysis of Successful Microfinance Programs." Rep. *Maximizing the Outreach of Microenterprise Finance: An Analysis of Successful Microfinance Programs.'* Washington, DC.

Christen, Robert Peck and Rosenberg, Richard. 2000. "The Rush to Regulate: Legal Frameworks for Microfinance." *CGAP Occasional Paper*, no. 4. Washington, DC: World Bank Accessed December 2, 2014. http://www.gdrc.org/icm/govern/regulation.pdf

Christen, Robert Peck and Deborah Drake. 2002. "Commercialization, the New Reality of Microfinance," In The Commercialization of Microfinance, Balancing Business and Development, edited by Deborah Drake and Elisabeth Rhyne, 2-22. Kumarian Press.

Collins, Daryl, Jonathan Morduch, Stuart Rutherford, Orlanda Ruthven. 2009. *Portfolios of the Poor: How the World's Poor Live on $2 a Day.* Princeton: Princeton University Press.

Conning, Jonathan. 1999. "Outreach, Sustainability and Leverage in Monitored and Peer-Monitored Lending." *Journal of Development Economics* 60 (1): 51–77. https://doi.org/10.1016/s0304-3878(99)00036-x.

Copestake, James. 2007. "Mainstreaming Microfinance: Social Performance Management or Mission Drift?" *World Development* 35 (10): 1721–38. https://doi.org/10.1016/j.worlddev.2007.06.004.

Correa, Amelia, and Romar Correa. 2009. "Microfinance: Equity and Debt Contracts." *Applied Economics Letters* 16 (8): 859–62. https://doi.org/10.1080/17446540802314501.

Cull, Robert, Asli Demirguc-Kunt, and Jonathan Morduch. 2007. "Financial Performance and Outreach: A Global Analysis of

Leading Microbanks." *Economic Journal* 117(517): 107-33 https://doi.org/10.1596/1813-9450-4630.

Cull, Robert, Asli Demirguc-Kunt, and Jonathan Morduch. 2009. "Microfinance Meets The Market." *Journal of Economic Perspectives* 23(1): 167-92 https://doi.org/10.1596/1813-9450-4630.

———. 2011. "Does Regulatory Supervision Curtail Microfinance Profitability and Outreach?" *World Development* 39 (6): 949–65. https://doi.org/10.1016/j.worlddev.2009.10.016.

Czura, Kristina. 2010. *An Impact Assessment of Microfinance in Sri lanka - A Household Survey of Microfinance Clients in 5 Selected GTZ Partner Microfinance.* 2-4. Frankfurt: Geoth University.

De Laiglesia, Juan Ramón. 2006. "Institutional Bottlenecks for Agricultural Development: A Stock-taking Exercise Based on Evidence from Sub-Saharan Africa." *OECD Development Centre Working Papers 248*, OECD Publishing.

Delfiner, M and S Peron. 2007, "Commercial Banks and Microfinance." *Munich Personal RePEc Archive Paper*, no. 10229. Accessed February 8, 2014. http://mpra.ub.uni-muenchen.de/10229/

Department of Census and Statistics. 1974. *World Population Year: Population of Sri Lanka.* Colombo: Department of Census and Statistics.

———. 2002. *Household Income and Expenditure Survey 2002.* Colombo: Department of Census and Statistics.

———. 2005. *Household Income and Expenditure Survey 2005.* Colombo: Department of Census and Statistics.

———. 2006/07. *Household Income and Expenditure Survey 2006/07.* Colombo: Department of Census and Statistics.

———. 2009/10. *Household Income and Expenditure Survey 2009/10.* Colombo: Department of Census and Statistics.

———. 2012/13. *Household Income and Expenditure Survey 2012/13.* Colombo: Department of Census and Statistics.

———. 2016. *Household Income and Expenditure Survey 2016.* Colombo: Department of Census and Statistics.

D'Espallier, Bert, Isabelle Guérin, and Roy Mersland. 2011. "Women and Repayment in Microfinance: A Global Analysis." *World Development* 39 (5): 758–72. https://doi.org/10.1016/j.worlddev.2010.10.008.

Dougherty, Christopher. 2016. *Introduction to Econometrics.* Oxford: Oxford University Press.

Dunham, David, and Sisira Jayasuriya. 2000. "Equity, Growth and Insurrection: Liberalization and the Welfare Debate in Contemporary Sri Lanka." *Oxford Development Studies* 28, no. 1: 97-110.

Field, Erica, and Rohini Pande. 2008. "Repayment Frequency and Default in Microfinance: Evidence from India." *Journal of the European Economic Association* 6 (2-3): 501–9. https://doi.org/10.1162/jeea.2008.6.2-3.501.

Floro, Maria Sagrario, and Debraj Ray. 1997. "Vertical Links Between Formal and Informal Financial Institutions." *Review of Development Economics* 1 (1): 34–56. https://doi.org/10.1111/1467-9361.00004.

Ghatak, Maitreesh. 1999. "Group Lending, Local Information and Peer Selection." *Journal of Development Economics* 60 (1): 27–50. https://doi.org/10.1016/s0304-3878(99)00035-8.

———. 2002. "Erratum to 'The Economics of Lending with Joint Liability: Theory and Practice' [J. Devel. Econ. 60 (1999) 195–228." *Journal of Development Economics* 69 (1): 305–6. https://doi.org/10.1016/s0304-3878(02)00064-0.

Godquin, Marie. 2004. "Microfinance Repayment Performance in Bangladesh: How to Improve the Allocation of Loans by MFIs." *World Development* 32 (11): 1909–26.

Gonzalez-Vega, Claudio, Mark Schreiner, Richard L. Meyer and Jorge Rodriguez. 1997. BancoSol: "The Challenge of Growth for Microfinance Organizations." *Occasional Paper*, no. 2332. Accessed February 2, 2012. http://www.microfinancegateway.org/content/article/detail/1420.

Gonzalez-Vega, C. 1998. "Microfinance: Broader Achievements and New Challenges." *Economics and Sociology, Occasional Paper*, no. 2518. Ohio State University.

Greenwood, Jeremy, and Boyan Jovanovic. 1990. "Financial Development, Growth, and the Distribution of Income." *Journal of Political Economy* 98 (5, Part 1): 1076–1107. https://doi.org/10.1086/261720.

Greene, William H. 2012. *Econometric Analysis*. Boston, MA: Pearson.

Gunatilaka, Ramani and Dulan De Silva. 2010. "Microfinance and Women's Empowerment: The Impact of Loan Ownership on

Women's Empowerment in Microfinance in Sri Lanka." *Centre for Women's Research* (CENWOR). Colombo.

Guttman, Joel M. 2007. Repayment Performance in Microcredit Programs: Theory and Evidence (March 2007). http://ssrn.com/abstract=985890 or http://dx.doi.org/10.2139/ssrn.985890.

———. 2008. "Assortative Matching, Adverse Selection, and Group Lending." *Journal of Development Economics* 87 (1): 51–56. https://doi.org/10.1016/j.jdeveco.2007.06.002.

Hannig, Alfred, and Stefan Jansen. 2010. "Financial Inclusion and Financial Stability: Current Policy Issues." *SSRN Electronic Journal.* https://doi.org/10.2139/ssrn.1729122.

Hardy, Daniel, Paul Holden, and Vassili Prokopenko. 2003. "Microfinance Institutions and Public Policy." *The Journal of Policy Reform* 6 (3): 147–58. https://doi.org/10.1080/13504850320001 75637.

Hartarska, Valentina, and Denis Nadolnyak. 2007. "Do Regulated Microfinance Institutions Achieve Better Sustainability and Outreach? Cross-Country Evidence." *Applied Economics* 39 (10): 1207–22. https://doi.org/10.1080/00036840500461840.

Haq, Mamiza, Mohammad Hoque and Shams Pathan. 2008. "Regulation of Microfinance Institutions in Asia: A Comparative Analysis." *International Review of Business Research Papers* 4(4): 421-450.

Herath, HMWA, LHP Gunaratne and Nimal Sanderatne. 2013. "Impact of Credit-plus Approach of Microfinance on Income Generation of Households." *Sri Lanka Journal of Economic Research* 1(1): 57-75.

Hermes, Niels, and Robert Lensink. 2007. "The Empirics of Microfinance: What Do We Know?" *The Economic Journal* 117 (517). https://doi.org/10.1111/j.1468-0297.2007.02013.x.

———. 2011. "Microfinance: Its Impact, Outreach, and Sustainability." *World Development* 39(6): 875–81. https://doi.org/10.1016/j.worlddev.2009.10.021.

Hermes, Niels, Robert Lensink, and Aljar Meesters. 2011. "Outreach and Efficiency of Microfinance Institutions." *World Development* 39(6): 938–48. https://doi.org/10.1016/j.worlddev.2009.10.018.

Hisako, Kai. 2009. "Competition and Wide Outreach of Microfinance Institutions." *Economics Bulletin* 29(4): 2628-2639.

Hishigsuren, Gaamaa. 2007. "Evaluating Mission Drift in Microfinance." *Evaluation Review* 31 (3): 203–60. https://doi.org/10.1177/0193841x06297886.

Hoff, Karla, and Joseph E. Stiglitz. 1998. "Moneylenders and Bankers: Price-Increasing Subsidies in a Monopolistically Competitive Market." *Journal of Development Economics* 55 (2): 485–518.

Holvoet, Nathalie. 2004. "Impact of Microfinance Programs on Children's Education, Do the Gender of the Borrower and the Delivery Model Matter?" *Journal of Microfinance* 6(2): 28-49.

Hsiao, Cheng. 2007. *Analysis of Panel Data*. Cambridge: Cambridge Univ. Press.

Hudak, Kristen. 2011. "The Capacity Dilemma: Regulating Microfinance in Sri Lanka and Nepal." *Journal of Banking Regulation* 13 (2): 99–113. https://doi.org/10.1057/jbr.2011.19.

Hudon, Marek, and Daniel Traca. 2011. "On the Efficiency Effects of Subsidies in Microfinance: An Empirical Inquiry." *World Development* 39 (6): 966–73. https://doi.org/10.1016/j.worlddev.2009.10.017.

Hulme, David and Paul Mosley.1996. *Finance against Poverty.* London: Routledge.

Hulme, David. 2000. "Is Micro Debt Good for Poor People? A Note on the Dark Side of Microfinance." *Small Enterprise Development* 11(1): 26-28.

Isenman, Paul. 1980. "Basic Needs: The Case of Sri Lanka." *World Development* 8, no. 3: 237-58.

Issahaku, Haruna, Stanley Kojo Dary, Ustarz Yazidu. 2013. "Financial Characteristics and Innovations in Microfinance Institutions in Ghana." *American Journal of Rural Development* 1(3): 40-48.

Jain, Sanjay, and Ghazala Mansuri. 2003. "A Little at a Time: The Use of Regularly Scheduled Repayments in Microfinance Programs." *Journal of Development Economics* 72, no. 1: 253-79.

Jalilian, Hossein, and Colin Kirkpatrick. 2005. "Does Financial Development Contribute to Poverty Reduction?" *Journal of Development Studies* 41, no. 4: 636-56.

Johnson, Susan, and Ben Rogaly. 1999. *Microfinance and Poverty Reduction.* Oxford, UK: Oxfam.

Karlan, Dean and Goldberg Nathanael. 2007. "Impact Evaluation for Microfinance: Review of Methodological Issues." *The World*

Bank Doing Impact Evaluation Series, no. 7. Washington, DC: World Bank.

Karlan, Dean and Jonathan Zinman. 2009. "Observing Unobservables: Identifying Information Asymmetries with a Consumer Credit Field Experiment." 2009. *Econometrica* 77 (6): 1993–2008. https://doi.org/10.3982/ecta5781.

Khatkhate, Deena. 1982. "Anatomy of Financial Retardation in a Less Developed Country: The Case of Sri Lanka, 1951–1976." *World Development* 10(9): 829–40.

King, Robert G., and Ross Levine. 1993a. "Finance and Growth: Schumpeter Might Be Right." *The Quarterly Journal of Economics* 108 (3): 717–37. https://doi.org/10.2307/2118406.

Kochar, Anjini. 1997. "An Empirical Investigation of Rationing Constraints in Rural Credit Markets in India." *Journal of Development Economics* 53 (2): 339–71.

Kono, Hisaki, and Kazushi Takahashi. 2010. "Microfinance Revolution: Its Effects, Innovations, And Challenges." *The Developing Economies* 48 (1): 15–73. https://doi.org/10.1111/j.1746-1049.2010.00098.x.

Kumar Kar, A. 2010. "Sustainability and Mission Drift in Microfinance." Thesis. Henken School of Economics.

Naveen Kumar, K. 2012. "Dynamic Incentives in Microfinance Group Lending." *SAGE Open* 2 (2):1-9. Accessed August 8, 2012. http://sgo.sagepub.com/content/2/2/2158244012444280

Laffont, J.J., and T N'Guessan. 2000. "Regulation and Development: Group Lending with Adverse Selection." *European Economic Review* 44(1):773-784.

Lanka Microfinance Practitioners' Association. 2012. *Microfinance Review - Sri Lanka, Performance and Analysis Report-2012.* Rajagiriya: Rathnayaka Enterprises.

Ledgerwood, Joanna. 1999. *Sustainable Banking with the Poor: Microfinance Handbook: an Institutional and Financial Perspective.* Washington, D.C.: World Bank.

Levine, Ross. 1997. "Financial Development and Economic Growth: Views and Agenda." *Journal of Economic Literature.* 35: 688-726.

Levine, Ross, Thorsten Beck, and Norman Loayza. 2000. "Finance and the Sources of Growth." *Journal of Financial Economics* 58 (1): 261-300.

Lucas, Robert E. 1988. "On the Mechanics of Economic Development." *Journal of Monetary Economics* 22 (1): 3–42. https://doi.org/10.1016/0304-3932(88)90168-7.

Luoto, Jill, Craig Mcintosh, and Bruce Wydick. 2007. "Credit Information Systems in Less Developed Countries: A Test with Microfinance in Guatemala." *Economic Development and Cultural Change* 55 (2): 313–34. https://doi.org/10.1086/508714.

Maddala, G.S. 2002. *Introduction to Econometrics.* New York:John Willey & Sons Ltd.

Mallick, Debdulal. 2012. "Microfinance and Moneylender Interest Rate: Evidence from Bangladesh." *World Development* 40(6): 1181–89. https://doi.org/10.1016/j.worlddev.2011.12.011.

McIntosh, Craig, and Bruce Wydick. 2005. "Competition and Microfinance." *Journal of Development Economics* 78 (2): 271–98.

McKinnon, Ronald I. 1973. *Money and Capital in Economic Development.* Washington, D.C.: Brookings Institution.

Mel, Suresh De, David Mckenzie, and Christopher Woodruff. 2009. "Are Women More Credit Constrained? Experimental Evidence on Gender and Microenterprise Returns." *American Economic Journal: Applied Economics* 1 (3): 1–32. https://doi.org/10.1257/app.1.3.1.

———. 2010. "Wage Subsidies for Microenterprises." *American Economic Review* 100 (2): 614–18. https://doi.org/10.1257/aer.100.2.614.

———. 2011. "Getting Credit to High Return Microentrepreneurs: The Results of an Information Intervention." *The World Bank Economic Review* 25 (3): 456–85. https://doi.org/10.1093/wber/lhr023.

Mersland, Roy. 2009. "The Cost of Ownership in Microfinance Organizations." *World Development* 37 (2): 469–78.

Mersland, Roy, and R. Øystein Strøm. 2009. "Performance and Governance in Microfinance Institutions." *Journal of Banking & Finance* 33(4): 662–69. https://doi.org/10.1016/j.jbankfin.2008.11.009.

———. 2010. "Microfinance Mission Drift?" *World Development* 38 (1): 28–36.

Meyer, Richard L. 2002. "The Demand for Flexible Microfinance Products: Lessons from Bangladesh." *Journal of International Development* 14(3):351–368.

Microfinance Information eXchange, 2010, *The MicroBanking Bulletin*, No.20. Washington DC:miX. Accessed December 02 2014. http://www.spandanaindia.com/pdfs/MBB202010.pdf

Microfinance Information eXchange. *What is Microfinance.* Washington DC:miX. Accessed December 02 2014. http://www.themix.org/about/microfinance

Ministry of Finance and Planning. 2018. *Annual Report.* Colombo: Ministry of Finance and Planning.

Montgomery, Heather, and John Weiss. 2011. "Can Commercially-Oriented Microfinance Help Meet the Millennium Development Goals? Evidence from Pakistan." *World Development* 39 (1): 87–109.

Morduch, Jonathan. 1999. "The Microfinance Promise." *Journal of Economic Literature* 37 (4): 1569-1614.

———. 2000. "The Microfinance Schism." *World Development* 28 (4): 617–29.

Morduch, Jonathan, Robert Cull, and Asli Demirguc-Kunt. 2006. "Financial Performance and Outreach: A Global Analysis of Leading Microbanks." *Policy Research Working Papers.* https://doi.org/10.1596/1813-9450-3827.

Mosley, Paul, and David Hulme. 1998. "Microenterprise Finance: Is There a Conflict between Growth and Poverty Alleviation?" *World Development* 26(5): 783–90.

Navajas, Sergio, Mark Schreiner, Richard L. Meyer, Claudio Gonzalez-Vega, and Jorge Rodriguez-Meza. 2000. "Microcredit and the Poorest of the Poor: Theory and Evidence from Bolivia." *World Development* 28 (2): 333–46.

Ngo, Thi Minh-Phuong, and Zaki Wahhaj. 2012. "Microfinance and Gender Empowerment." *Journal of Development Economics* 99(1): 1–12.

Odedokun, M.O. 1996. "Alternative Econometric Approaches for Analysing the Role of the Financial Sector in Economic Growth: Time-Series Evidence from LDCs." *Journal of Development Economics* 50 (1): 119–46.

Olivare-Polanco, F. 2005. "Commercializing Microfinance and Deepening Outreach? Empirical Evidence from Latin America." *Journal of Microfinance/ESR Review* 7(2): 47-69.

Oscar, Torres-Reyna. n.d. "Panel Data Analysis Fixed & Random Effects (using Stata 10.x)." Accessed October 1, 2013. http://www.princeton.edu/~otorres/Panel101.pdf.

Panda, Debadutta K. 2010. *Understanding Microfinance*. New Delhi: Wiley India.

Paxton, Julia. 2003. "A Poverty Outreach Index and its Application to Microfinance." *Economics Bulletin* 9(2): 1-10.

Pitt, Mark M., and Shahidur R. Khandker. 1998. "The Impact of Group-Based Credit Programs on Poor Households in Bangladesh: Does the Gender of Participants Matter?" *Journal of Political Economy* 106 (5): 958–96. https://doi.org/10.1086/250037. -96.

Porteous, D. 2006. "Competition and Microcredit Interest Rates." *CGAP Focus Note*, no. 33, Washington, DC: World Bank.

Premaratne, S.P. 2002. "Access to Capital: A Comparison of Men and Women Owned Small Business in Sri Lanka." *Sri Lanka Economic Journal* 3(2): 32-55.

————. "Accessibility and Affordability of Rural Microfinance Services in Sri Lanka." *Sri Lanka Economic Journal* 10(2): 109-136.

Premaratne, S.P., S.M.P Senanayake and M Warnasuriya. 2012. "Empowerment of Women through Self Help Groups (SHGs): A Study of a SHG Microfinance Project in Sri Lanka." *UEH Journal of Economic Development* 210: 17-36.

Quayes, Shakil. 2012. "Depth of Outreach and Financial Sustainability of Microfinance Institutions." *Applied Economics* 44(26): 3421–33. https://doi.org/10.1080/00036846.2011.577016.

Rai, Ashok, and Shamika Ravi. 2011. "Do Spouses Make Claims? Empowerment and Microfinance in India." *World Development* 39 (6): 913–21.

Rhyne E. 1998. "The Yin and Yang of Microfinance: Reaching the Poor and Sustainability." *MicroBanking Bulletin* 2: 6-9.

Robinson, Joan. 1952. "The Generalisation of the General Theory." In *The Rate of Interest and Other Essays,* edited by Joan Robinson, PPP, London: MacMillan.

Robinson, Marguerite. 1994b. "Savings Mobilization and Microenterprise Finance: The Indonesian Experience." In *The New World of Microenterprise Finance: Building Healthy Financial Institutions for the Poor,* edited by Otero María, and Elisabeth Rhyne, PPP, West Hartford, CT: Kumarian Press.

————. 2001. *The Microfinance Revolution: Sustainable Finance for the Poor.* Washington D.C.: World Bank.

Rosengard, Jay K. 2004. "Banking on Social Entrepreneurship: The Commercialization of Microfinance." *Mondes En Développement* 126 (2): 25-36. https://doi.org/10.3917/med.126.0025.

Sagamba, Moïse, Oleg Shchetinin, and Nurmukhammad Yusupov. 2013. "Do Microloan Officers Want to Lend to the Less Advantaged? Evidence from a Choice Experiment." *World Development* 42: 182–98.

Sanderatne, Nimal. 1982. "A Profile of the Informal Rural Credit Markets in Mid Seventies." *Staff Studies, Central Bank of Sri Lanka* 11(182): 20-35.

———. 2004. "Interest Rates and Financial Viability of Microfinance." *Bankers Journal* xxiii (02/03): 46-50.

Schreiner, Mark. 2002. "Aspects of Outreach: a Framework for Discussion of the Social Benefits of Microfinance." *Journal of International Development* 14(5): 591–603.

Schumpeter, Joseph A. 1991. *The Theory of Economic Development.* Cambridge: Harvard University Press.

Sen, Amartya. 1981. *Poverty and Famines: An Essay on Entitlement and Deprivation.* Oxford: Clarendon Press.

———. 2009. "Public Action And The Quality Of Life In Developing Countries*." *Oxford Bulletin of Economics and Statistics* 43 (4): 287–319. https://doi.org/10.1111/j.1468-0084.1981.mp43004001.x.

Senanayake, SMP. 2002. "An Overview of the Microfinance Sector in Sri Lanka." *Savings and Development* 26(2):197-222.

————. 2003. "Some Critical Issues Relating to the Commercialization of Micro Finance Sector in Sri Lanka." *Savings and Development* 27(2): 79-95.

Senanayake, SMP. and SP Premaratne. 2006. "Microfinance for Accelerated Development." Savings *and Development* 30(2): 143-168.

Sengupta, Rajdeep, and Craig P. Aubuchon. 2008. "The Microfinance Revolution: An Overview." *Federal Reserve Bank of St. Louis Review* 90(1): 9-30.

Serrano-Cinca, Carlos, and Begoña Gutiérrez-Nieto. 2014. "Microfinance, the Long Tail and Mission Drift." *International Business Review* 23(1): 181–94. https://doi.org/10.1016/j.ibusrev.2013.03.006.

Shankar, S and MG Asher. 2010. "Regulating Microfinance: A Suggested Framework." *Economic and Political Weekly* 45(1): 15-18.

Shaw, Edward Stone. 1973. *Financial Deepening in Economic Development.* New York, NY: Oxford University Press.

Shaw, Judith. 2004. "Microenterprise Occupation and Poverty Reduction in Microfinance Programs: Evidence from Sri Lanka." *World Development* 32 (7): 1247–64.

Simtowe, Franklin, Manfred Zeller, and Alexander Phiri. 2006. "Determinants of Moral Hazard in Microfinance: Empirical Evidence from Joint Liability Lending Schemes in Malawi." 2006 Annual Meeting, August 12-18, 2006, Queensland, Australia 25287: International Association of Agricultural Economists.

Simtowe, Franklin Peter, and Manfred Zeller. 2006. "Determinants of Intra-Group Insurance in Microfinance: Evidence from Joint

Liability Lending Programs in Malawi." *SSRN Electronic Journal.* https://doi.org/10.2139/ssrn.939333.

Sriram, MS. 2005. "Information Asymmetry and Trust: A Framework for Studying Microfinance in India." *Vikalpa* 30(04): 77-85.

Stiglitz, Joseph E. and Andrew Weiss. 1981. "Credit Rationing in Markets with Imperfect Information." *American Economic Review* 71(3): 393-410.

Stiglitz, Joseph E. 1994. "The Role of the State in Financial Markets." In Bruno Michael and Boris Pleskovic, eds., *Proceeding of the World Bank Annual Conference on Development Economics, 1993: Supplement to the World Bank Economic Review and the World Bank Research Observer.* Washington, DC: World Bank.

Stiglitz, Joseph E. 2000. "Capital Market Liberalization, Economic Growth, and Instability." *World Development* 28 (6): 1075–86.

Stock, James H., and Mark W. Watson. 2020. *Introduction to Econometrics.* Harlow, England: Pearson.

Tassel, Eric Van. 1999. "Group Lending under Asymmetric Information." *Journal of Development Economics* 60 (1): 3–25.

Tedeschi, Gwendolyn Alexander. 2006. "Here Today, Gone Tomorrow: Can Dynamic Incentives Make Microfinance More Flexible?" *Journal of Development Economics* 80 (1): 84–105.

Tilakaratna, Ganga, Upali Wickramasinghe and Thusitha Kumara. 2005. Microfinance in Sri Lanka: A Household Level Analysis of Outreach and Impact on Poverty. Colombo: Institute of Policy Studies.

Tucker, Michael. 2001. "Financial Performance of Selected Microfinance Institutions, Benchmarking Progress to Sustainability." *Journal of Microfinance* 3(2): 108-123.

Vanroose, Annabel, and Bert D'Espallier. 2013. "Do Microfinance Institutions Accomplish Their Mission? Evidence from the Relationship between Traditional Financial Sector Development and Microfinance Institutions' Outreach and Performance." *Applied Economics* 45 (15): 1965–82. https://doi.org/10.1080/00036846.20 11.641932.

Von Stauffenberg, Damian. 2003. "Definitions of Selected Financial Terms, Ratios, and Adjustments for Microfinance (English). Microfinance Consensus Guidelines." Rep. *Definitions of Selected Financial Terms, Ratios, and Adjustments for Microfinance (English). Microfinance Consensus Guidelines.* Washington: World Bank.

Wachtel, Paul. 2001. "Growth and Finance: What Do We Know and How Do We Know It?" *International Finance* 4 (3): 335–62.

Weiss, John, and Heather Montgomery. 2005. "Great Expectations: Microfinance and Poverty Reduction in Asia and Latin America." *Oxford Development Studies* 33 (3-4): 391–416.

Woller, Garry, Dunford Christopher and Warner Woodworth. 1999. "Where to microfinance?", *International Journal of Economic Development* (1): 29-64.

Woller, Gary. 2002. "The Promise and Peril of Microfinance Commercialization." *Small Enterprise Development* 13 (4): 12–21.

World Bank. 2006. "*The CGAP CLEAR Review of 2006.*" Accessed August 4, 2014. http://documents.worldbank.org/curated/en/2006/02/6726134/ sri-lanka-country-level-effectiveness-accountability-review.

Yaron, Jacob. 1992. *Rural Finance in Developing Countries*, WPS No. 875. Agriculture and Rural Development Department, World Bank. Washington DC.

Zeller, Manfred. 2003. Models of Rural Financial institutions. Lead Theme Paper at Paving the Way Forward for Rural Finance: An International Conference on Best Practices, Washington, D.C., June 2-4, 2003. www.woccu.org.

ABOUT THE AUTHOR

Dr. Amarathunga, who has been with the Central Bank of Sri Lanka (CBSL) over 30 years, currently holds the position of director of the bank's Regional Office Management Department. Apart from attending his main job, he has functioned as a member of the committees tasked with the preparation of policy and strategy documents on SMEs and venture capital firms in Sri  Lanka, as a trustee of dedicated economic centers and as a board member of country's premier institute for agrarian research and training. Dr. Amarathunga was also a member of presidential task force for the recovery of state assets during 2015-17, chairman of the Bay of Bengal Initiative for Multi-Sectoral Technical and Economic Cooperation (BIMSTEC) sub group on countering the financing of terrorism in 2015, and co-chair of the Asia Pacific Group on Money Laundering (APG) during 2016-17.

Before joining the CBSL, Dr. Amarathunga worked as an Assistant Lecturer of the University of Peradeniya, Sri Lanka, from where he received his B.Com. (special) degree and later, while serving in the CBSL, he completed MSc in Economic and Social Policy Analysis from the University of York, MSc in Management and Information Technology from the University of Kelaniya, Sri Lanka and PhD in Microfinance from the University of Colombo, Sri Lanka.

He has published research papers in reputed journals. He is also a resource person for many local and international training programs conducted on Regional Development, Money Laundering and Terrorist Financing.

INDEX

Printed in the United States
By Bookmasters